Break Free From Over Thinking

Break Free From Over Thinking

5 Spiritual Tools to Reclaim Your Peace of Mind

Vraja Bihari Das

JAICO PUBLISHING HOUSE

Ahmedabad Bangalore Chennai
Delhi Hyderabad Kolkata Mumbai

Published by Jaico Publishing House
A-2 Jash Chambers, 7-A Sir Phirozshah Mehta Road
Fort, Mumbai - 400 001
jaicopub@jaicobooks.com
www.jaicobooks.com

BREAK FREE FROM OVERTHINKING
ISBN 978-81-990707-3-8

First Jaico Impression: 2025

Page design and layout by Jojy Philip, Delhi

Printed by
Nutech Print Services - India, New Delhi

To my seniors, mentors, and friends in the monastery who taught me how to overcome overthinking.

Contents

Introduction

> *"One should not let one's mind be overcome by dismay. Melancholy destroys a man just as an angered serpent kills an innocent child."*
>
> —*Ramayana* (Kishkindha Kanda, 64.9)

"How did you end up marrying this rascal? Of all the eligible bachelors, why him?" I asked Krishangi, surprised. Laughter erupted as everyone enjoyed the playful exchange. Krishangi blushed while her husband, Milind, protested with a grin. "What do you mean? I'm quite handsome and well-educated," he said with a chuckle. "I'm definitely deserving of her as a wife! She couldn't have asked for a better deal in life."

More relatives joined in, teasing the couple. Milind, my best friend's son, has been a part of my life since he was a toddler. Krishangi embodies grace, and while she exudes beauty and charm, her choice of Milind—despite his contrasting mannerisms—amused many friends and relatives.

"I may not be as refined as she is but I love her deeply, and she knows it," he declared proudly in his characteristic, unpolished manner. Milind's golden heart has always reflected care and chivalry since his school days. "Naturally, his courage and love must have won her heart," a relative said, defending Milind's selection by the noble Krishangi. Another friend quipped, “He’s an introvert, and maybe the physics rule of ‘like poles repel and unlike poles attract’ is at play here.”

The newlyweds hosted a spiritual gathering at a temple. Blessings from family and friends flowed in, along with good-natured teasing. Krishangi found herself explaining her choice of husband, and her words delighted me, reaffirming my own relationship with God, whom we in ISKCON worship as Krishna, the youthful and all-attractive Supreme Personality of Godhead.

“I met Milind during my first year of medical school, and it certainly wasn’t love at first sight,” Krishangi clarified. “We first crossed paths at a common friend’s birthday party and discovered we were in the same class. From then on, we frequently interacted at college and at various social gatherings. Over the years, I saw him support and care for me in many ways—helping with my studies, quietly empathizing with my insecurities, and comforting me during conflicts with roommates and friends. He spoke little but was always attentive to my worries, big and small. He offered advice sparingly, only when I was open to it. By the time our medical internship ended, after seven years of knowing each other, I was convinced he truly loved me. And then, I don’t know exactly when or how, but I also fell in love with him.”

My heart resonated with every word Krishangi spoke. My own love story with God was quite similar. Plagued by overthinking and worry, I found solace when Krishna—the all-attractive Supreme Personality of Godhead in Hindu tradition—entered my life. I first encountered the Lord through the pages of my morning journal. Initially, I wasn’t moved by Krishna, but the practice of Bhakti-Yoga gradually won me over. As I poured out my paralyzing thoughts into my journal daily, I felt as though God, much like Milind in Krishangi's case, was lending me a sympathetic ear.

Meanwhile, at the marriage reception, as cheers filled the air, a friend playfully hummed a popular Bollywood song where the heroine sings to the hero, *"Na na karte pyaar tumi se kar baithe, karna tha inkar magar ikrar tumi se kar baithe."* This translates loosely to, "I kept saying no, but I don't know when and how I fell in love with you. I wanted to reject you but ended up saying yes." The song perfectly echoed Krishangi's journey that led to her marriage with Milind.

The song was an epiphany for me. I joined the monastery over a quarter century ago, and I was younger, passionate, and ambitious. I was externally a monk apprentice but internally far away from what a *sadhu*—a monk should be. I also don't believe I loved Krishna, God, as deeply back then.

I was beset with overthinking. I worried about whether my parents were okay, whether my brothers would disown me for severing family ties, whether my authorities in the monastery would recognize my sincerity in spiritual pursuits, and whether I was making spiritual progress. I questioned whether I had made the right decision by joining the ashram. And then, I was overthinking about my overthinking!

Externally, I maintained a brave, 'all's well' demeanor, but internally, I was anxious and in need of respite. During this time, I began maintaining a gratitude journal, where I expressed thanks for both small and large gifts daily. I thanked God, friends, and my spiritual teachers, and appreciated others for the goodness they brought into my life. Sometimes, my journal felt like a dry ritual as my mind dwelled on the numerous problems in my life. Yet I persevered, recognizing how God orchestrated wonderful gifts and silently guided me in my heart, allowing me to pursue my interests. Despite the ups and downs of life, my gratitude journal persisted, and the practice of expressing gratitude endured. Even with brief interruptions and deviations, I always returned to this practice. The entire journey was similar to Krishangi's—I realized God is always available for me. He is quiet, attentive, and also non-judgmental.

One early morning, as I meticulously listed the ten beautiful gifts God had bestowed upon me in the past twenty-four hours, I was overwhelmed with emotion. A sudden, intuitive realization struck me—a simple yet profound truth: God indeed loves me. Tears welled up in my eyes, and my entire life flashed before me. In that moment, I felt that I was enveloped in causeless mercy.

In this illuminating discovery, I witnessed grace flow even towards a friend-turned-foe. A few years ago, serious differences had strained our friendship to the point of ending communication. I had harbored resentment, but now, in this moment of realizing God's love, I felt forgiveness and love surging through me. I was stunned, and somehow, I knew that I had either fallen—or perhaps risen—in love with Krishna.

Through my gratitude journal, I began to see how God (Krishna) had been consistently there for me. Like Krishangi, I faced worries, conflicts, and needs. Navigating the internal trials of my mind and the external challenges of monastic life, I observed Krishna—much like Milind—always offering silent support.

One day, in a moment of deep love and gratitude, an unintended sentence slipped into my journal: "Krishna, you have done so much for me; I also want to serve you in a way that will truly make you happy. Please guide me on how I can serve you."

Though inadvertent, this sentence marked my entry—albeit brief—into a transcendental dimension. Bhakti-Yoga teaches that authentic prayer and connection with God begin when we ask gifts not for ourselves but inquire about how we can serve the Lord. It was a genuine outpouring of a heart steeped in thankfulness.

In that moment, I realized that my worries were insignificant, Krishna was real, and my relationship with Him was eternal. Despite my frequent lapses into overthinking and illusion, and acknowledging my shortcomings in spiritual life, I understood that I had found my true companion. Aware of my inadequacies, I found joy in my relationship with God. Though not pure, my gratitude practices kept me sincere. Despite making mistakes, I felt reassured by the Lord that I am not a mistake! I had finally found someone who would never judge me, accept me as I am, and gently guide me to explore my full spiritual potential. He was always witnessing and willing to guide me, provided I was willing to listen.

Just as Krishangi found her soulmate in Milind, Bhakti-Yoga practitioners find Lord Krishna as their ever-supportive companion. Krishangi chose Milind when she realized he loved her unconditionally; similarly, a spiritual practitioner chooses God when they recognize His love in their heart. God loves us, and when we connect to His love through the practices mentioned in this book, we move from overthinking to effective and productive thinking.

I am now convinced that the spiritual solution to overthinking is grounded in gratitude. Practicing gratitude (which we will explore in greater depth in Chapters 4 and 5) can help us forge a deeper, more fulfilling relationship with the universe, which is always conspiring to elevate us to higher levels of spiritual awakening. Gratitude is one of the most powerful spiritual tools that can help us transition from the quicksand of overthinking to the spiritual grove of abundance and happiness.

This book is my humble attempt to share the power, magic, and hope that the five tools—easily remembered as A.B.C.D.E—can bring to our lives.

A Stands for Three A's -Awareness, Acceptance, and Action

In Chapter 1, we will discuss the tool of the three A's and understand the five sheaths that cover our real identity, as explained in the *Upanishads*. We will discover how overthinking arises in the mind and learn to separate ourselves from our thoughts, accepting and allowing them to exist without judgment. Counterintuitive as it may seem, allowing the mind to overthink a problem while maintaining a separate identity from it can deflate the mind's incessant chatter. Besides, we will see the most practical method—'Action' of service which instantly punctures the overthinking disease.

B Is Breathe

One of the most underutilized human resources is our breath. Simply inhaling oxygen and exhaling carbon dioxide, slowly and consciously, can lead to immediate and dramatic improvements in mental well-being. In Chapter 2, we will delve into the subject of relaxation and conscious breathing and its role in addressing overthinking.

C Stands for Chant

Chanting mantras softly on beads, a practice rooted in Indian tradition, may seem simple but holds profound spiritual potential. Chanting can elevate us to a state beyond the mind. The key is to be present and prayerful, and listen to the sound vibrations. As we chant mindfully, we connect with the deeper spiritual feelings that transcend the physical sound. Chapter 3 will explore the dynamics of sound, thoughts, and feelings, and how chanting sacred mantras can rewire our neural pathways to break free from overthinking and help us envision a better future.

D Is Diary

Overthinking is essentially our mind's incessant chatter. Journaling or keeping a daily diary offers a way to quiet this babble by providing a space for the mind to express its concerns. By objectively noting down our thoughts, we can slow them down and gain distance from them. In Chapter 4, we will explore over seven different journaling techniques and how they can create mental space to better address our problems. Currently, many of us use our brains to store problems rather than solve them. Journaling acts like a video camera for our inner world, giving us greater control over our thoughts by presenting them factually and without emotional distortion.

E Stands for Energy

The energy of blessings, gratitude, and appreciation can be a game changer. Uplifting and glorifying others is a powerful remedy for a self-obsessed mind. Overthinking often feeds on negative loops of fear, anxiety, and regret. A culture of gratitude and appreciation shifts our focus from scarcity to abundance. By recognizing and celebrating the successes of others, we move beyond ourselves and unleash a powerful spiritual energy within and around us. In Chapter 5, we will learn the art of creating a better future for ourselves by practicing a goodness-centered life, by studying scriptures, and by appreciating others.

Some terms used repeatedly in this book may seem unfamiliar to the reader. The phrase "Krishna consciousness" refers to a state of spiritual awareness or divine consciousness. "Devotional service" denotes the practice of Bhakti-Yoga. I include numerous anecdotes and teachings from the lives of His Holiness Radhanath Swami (my spiritual master) and Srila Prabhupada, the founder-acharya of ISKCON (the International Society for Krishna Consciousness). Additionally, I share stories from the monastery where I have lived for the past two and a half decades. As I serve the worldwide ISKCON community and travel extensively, I encounter many interesting people and learn valuable lessons, which I have also shared here, though I have altered names to protect their identities.

The teachings presented by the Bhakti-Yoga tradition and ISKCON are neither sectarian nor intended to be preachy. Instead, they offer a different perspective on overthinking—a model grounded in the ancient wisdom of the Vedic literatures like the *Upanishads,* the *Bhagavad Gita,* the *Śrīmad-Bhāgavatam,* the *Mahabharata,* and the *Ramayana.* These scriptures are universal in their teachings, and their life lessons remain as relevant today as they were millennia ago.

Following in the footsteps of my predecessors in the Bhakti-Yoga tradition, I have humbly attempted to make spiritual life accessible to the modern busy man and woman.

I request you to overlook my shortcomings and consider this book as a sincere effort to share heartfelt insights on the subject of overthinking. I am deeply grateful to you for picking up this book.

I earnestly pray that you see the weed of negative thinking uprooted from your divine heart, and that the seed of gratitude blossoms into a beautiful tree of love for God. May this spiritual love inspire us all to bring happiness to the planet.

> *"Overthinking is when memories are stored in the mind,*
> *but gratitude is when memories are stored in the heart."*
> —Lionel Hampton

Part A

Awareness

CHAPTER 1

Three A's – Awareness, Acceptance, and Action

> *"O son of Prtha (Arjuna), do not yield to this degrading impotence. It does not become you. Give up such petty weakness of heart and arise, O chastiser of the enemy."*
>
> —*The Bhagavad Gita* (2.2)

At thirty-five, I was an abrasive monk, earnest in my desire to help a suffering soul. Yet when I admitted a young man struggling with alcohol and drug addiction into a rehabilitation center against his will, anxiety gripped me. My intentions were sincere—I wanted to save him—but my actions were impulsive.

The questions and fears came rushing in: *What if everything went wrong? Where would I get the funds? How long would the treatment last? Who would care for him after? What if he retaliated, and my efforts backfired?*

Though my heart was in the right place, doubt and overthinking consumed me. In my search for relief, I turned to distractions—comfort food, music, YouTube, social media—but none provided lasting peace. They merely dulled the ache temporarily while the painful reality continued to stare me down. My heart pounded, blood pressure rose, and my nervousness intensified.

The solution, I knew, was simple: *pause, breathe, pray, and engage in meaningful action.* Yet my restless mind—whom I call *Chanchal* (meaning restless or fickle)—refused to cooperate. Its panicked wails and obstinate refusal to embrace reality left me paralyzed.

But days passed in endless melancholy. I wondered if even I needed to get admitted in that center as I saw myself sink into an abyss. Life sucked.

One evening, as Chanchal's panic peaked and I instinctively reached for my phone to drown in YouTube's comforting chaos, I stopped. I mustered all my strength to do nothing—yes, *do nothing.* It took effort, but I turned off my phone and closed my eyes.

I sat with the pain. No reading, no music, no calls to friends, no scrolling. I was alone with my misery. And yet, paradoxically, a strange peace began to emerge. I realized my fear and anxiety had been magnified by constant distractions. Alone with my pain, I discovered it wasn't as overwhelming as I had imagined.

This moment was the genesis of my practice of *awareness* and *acceptance.*

I told myself: "I am in pain. I accept this pain. I allow it to reside within me."

I got specific: "I am aware that Chanchal is unhappy and deeply worried." This small but deliberate acknowledgment is called *awareness*, and it pulled me out of the mind's overthinking spiral. For the first time, I glimpsed freedom from its relentless grip.

Next, I embraced *acceptance*: "I accept Chanchal's anxiety and worry. It is okay, my dear Chanchal, to feel miserable. It is not your fault. You have lived in fear for so long, and now you are anxious. That's okay."

This acceptance felt liberating. Slowly, I rose with quiet determination. I slipped on my shoes and went for a brisk evening walk. As I moved, my mind cleared, and the endorphins from the walk lifted my spirits. I returned refreshed, free from the suffocating sadness. This was *action* in action!

That evening, I discovered the power of the three A's:

1. **Awareness** – Recognize and name your emotions without judgment.
2. **Acceptance** – Allow your feelings to exist without resistance.
3. **Action** – Take meaningful, restorative steps forward.

Together, these tools provided a roadmap to navigate overthinking and regain inner peace.

Let us now delve into the essence of each of these three transformative steps: awareness, acceptance, and action.

#1 What Are the Three A's – Awareness, Acceptance, and Action?

Awareness

> *"One who sees inaction in action, and action in inaction, is intelligent among men, and he is in the transcendental position, although engaged in all sorts of activities.""*
>
> —*The Bhagavad Gita* (4.18)

Awareness is the ability to observe yourself without judgment. It is the foundation for transformation, the first step in breaking free from the autopilot mode of life.

Imagine this: You binge on chocolates after a stressful day. You could either berate yourself for slipping from your dietary standards or justify the indulgence, claiming it is your choice. But if you pause and notice a recurring pattern—grabbing chocolates or binge-watching Netflix whenever you feel lonely—you are demonstrating *awareness*.

Most of us respond automatically to life: hunger prompts us to eat, anger makes us yell, and sadness leads to indulgence. These are habitual responses with no space between the trigger and our reaction. Awareness creates that space. It allows you to observe your life from a vantage point, enabling you to choose your responses consciously rather than reacting impulsively.

In the spiritual tradition I follow, monks dedicate two hours daily to meditation. We rise early, chant the holy names of God together, and reflect in stillness. Over time, this consistent practice reveals the chaotic voices in our minds.

The first lesson we learn through *awareness* is this: *"I am not my mind. I am not my thoughts."*

The demon and the divine

Picture this: A ten-foot-tall, ferocious demon with horns, red eyes, sharp teeth, and razor-like claws stands by your side 24/7. On your other side, a radiant, calm, loving figure—representing God or your higher self—is patiently waiting.

The demon is your mind. It screams at you to eat chocolate when you're lonely. Later, it chastises you for eating recklessly.

Then, it frightens you with thoughts of diabetes. Its relentless cycle of cajoling, blaming, and scolding never stops.

Most of us live as slaves to this demon. Its words feel urgent and important, and we blindly obey its commands. Ironically, this demon is harmless—it cannot physically touch you. It is not even *you*!

Awareness begins when you observe this demon from a distance. You might say:

- *"My mind is telling me to grab a chocolate."*
- *"Now my mind is scolding me for eating the chocolate."*
- *"Now my mind is worried I'll get diabetes."*

This separation is the key. When you stop identifying with the mind's constant chatter, you step into a space of *awareness*. You realize the demon is simply a noisy neighbor, not a master to be obeyed.

Turning to the Divine

On your right, the Divine—or your higher self—waits patiently. This presence embodies peace, love, and wisdom, but you often ignore it because you're too engrossed in the mind's drama. The path to true freedom lies in turning away from the demon and toward this higher presence.

Awareness is your compass. It helps you recognize the mind's manipulations and guides you toward the quiet, merciful embrace of the Divine.

The practice of awareness

To cultivate *awareness*, pause and observe:

- *What is my mind saying right now?*
- *How is it influencing my actions?*
- *Can I create space between my thoughts and my response?*

When you separate yourself from the mind's relentless chatter, you reclaim your power. From this space, transformation becomes possible. The demon loses its grip, and the higher, wiser part of you takes the lead.

The *Svetasvatara Upanishad* (4.7) and the *Mundaka Upanishad* (3.1.1-2), ancient Sanskrit texts from the Vedas, poetically describe our relationship with God:

> *"There are two birds on the same tree—the eating bird and the observing bird. The eating bird is engrossed with anxiety and moroseness as the enjoyer of the fruits of the tree. But if in some way, he turns his face to his friend, the peaceful bird, who is the Lord, at once the suffering bird becomes free from all anxieties."*

We are like the eating bird, captivated by the fruits of the material world. Each bite into the pleasures or pains of worldly actions drags us deeper into an endless cycle of suffering. Yet, every so often, we glimpse the peaceful bird—the Supreme Lord, residing in our hearts—and long to connect with Him.

However, just as we prepare to fly to His branch, another tempting fruit catches our eye. We pause, reconsider, and tell ourselves, "Just one last attempt to find joy here." But the material world repeatedly disappoints us, leaving us stuck in this cycle of longing and disillusionment.

Only when we finally turn to the peaceful bird, our eternal friend, do our miseries end. The rest of this book is devoted to learning how to turn toward Him—by taming the mind's incessant chatter and making choices that arise from awareness rather than impulsive desires.

Awareness is a gift that comes when we pause and slow down. In stillness, we notice the mind urging us to binge on chocolates or scroll through Netflix. Awareness gives us the space to recognize the mind's impulses instead of being helplessly dragged along by them.

But awareness alone is not enough.

Acceptance

> *"Surrender and accept Him exclusively, with your whole being, O Bharat. By His grace, you will attain perfect peace and eternal abode."*
>
> —*The Bhagavad Gita* (18.62)

The mind is crafty and manipulative. It will shift tactics, sneaking in through the back door, saying, "Your mind is bad. You're hopeless. You're wasting your life. You'll die of diabetes. What's the point of trying?"

Do you see what's happening? The mind cleverly disguises itself as your higher self, using the language of self-criticism and despair to keep you bound.

This is why *acceptance* is essential.

Acceptance is a non-judgmental acknowledgment of the mind's voice. Instead of resisting or fighting it, you embrace its presence without letting it control you:

- *"My mind is urging me to grab a chocolate. I accept this desire without judgment."*
- *"My mind is angry that I indulged. I accept its anger."*

Acceptance creates distance between you and the mind's emotional games. When you accept what the mind says without resistance, you disarm its power. The emotions lose their grip, and you stop reacting impulsively.

It is like shifting from being an actor in a drama to being the video camera recording it. A camera observes without emotion; it simply captures. Similarly, *acceptance* allows you to observe the mind clinically, without getting entangled in its drama.

From mind's noise to God's voice

When you practice *awareness* and *acceptance*, you puncture the relentless rant of the mind. The demon quietens down, like a tantrum-throwing child who realizes they have been caught. In that silence, you can finally turn to your right, where your best friend and eternal well-wisher—God, Krishna, or your higher self—has been patiently waiting.

His voice is soft, gentle, and reassuring—a stark contrast to the mind's loud, chaotic chatter. However, until now, the noise of the mind has drowned Him out.

Through *awareness* and *acceptance*, you create the space to hear Him.

In Chapter 5, we will again study *awareness* and *acceptance* in the context of developing a goodness-centered life.

The final step: Action

The mind remains sneaky and relentless. Even with *awareness* and *acceptance*, its exhausting pull can return. Therefore, we need to invoke *action*.

Action transforms insight into reality. While *awareness* and *acceptance* quieten the mind, meaningful *action* keeps you grounded in the present moment, ensuring the mind has less room to maneuver. Together, these three—*awareness, acceptance, and action*—are keys to overcoming the mind's distractions and reconnecting with your true self and the divine within.

Action

> *"O son of Kunti, either you will be killed on the battlefield and attain the heavenly planets, or you will conquer and enjoy the earthly kingdom. Therefore, get up with determination and fight."*
>
> —*The Bhagavad Gita* (2.37)

Arjuna, a warrior undefeated in battle, finds himself paralyzed with doubt at the cusp of the greatest war of his life. His overthinking leads him to propose an absurd solution to Krishna: abandoning the battlefield to live as a beggar in the forest. Krishna sharply rebukes Arjuna for his "mental impotence," reminding him that his duty is to act without attachment to results.

Krishna's message is crystal clear: Action is the solution for the mind's relentless overthinking and catastrophizing. The mind has a peculiar tendency to inflate minor problems into monumental crises, leading to inaction or misguided decisions—like Arjuna's initial impulse to flee. Ironically, such avoidance often turns small issues into far bigger ones.

Overthinking vs. Action

Overthinking traps us in a cycle of mental hyperactivity while keeping the body inactive. The mind convinces us that we're engaged in an important introspection when, in truth, we're just running in mental circles. It flatters us: "You're a deep thinker, a reflective and sincere person. Keep pondering, and you'll eventually discover the ultimate solution to all your problems."

However, thinking doesn't always lead to knowing. Two clear signs of overthinking are:

1. **Repetition without resolution:** You keep revisiting the same issues without any clarity or progress.
2. **Lack of tangible action:** Despite all the mental effort, no practical steps are taken to address the issue.

This cycle leaves the brain fatigued, the body inert, and the spirit miserable.

Action, however, shatters the mind's deceptive loop. By engaging in meaningful, practical activities, we disrupt the mental inertia and restore clarity and focus.

The transformative power of service

During my early years as a monk-apprentice, I accompanied my senior to a weekly *Bhagavad Gita* class at a medical college hostel. One of the attendees, Dilip, was an overthinker par excellence. He bombarded my senior with endless questions, often repetitive, barely waiting for answers before launching into the next query. His mind seemed to be running on overdrive, and his questions often reflected the chaos within.

One day, after yet another exhausting session, my senior interrupted Dilip mid-question. "Why don't you do something practical?" he suggested. "Next month, we're organizing our annual eye and dental camp in the villages of North India. Many medical students and doctors volunteer to serve. Why don't you join us and gain some new experiences?"

Dilip readily agreed and joined us for the eight-week service program. Each day, he rose early for prayers, participated in community practices, and assisted the medical team. He helped elderly villagers settle in for cataract surgeries, counseled young villagers, and rendered menial but heartfelt service. His days were filled with activity, connection, and purpose.

Two months later, we resumed the weekly *Bhagavad Gita* class. At the end of the session, my senior asked for questions. All eyes turned to Dilip, expecting his usual barrage. Instead, he sat quietly, radiating a calm, contented smile.

Curious, I nudged him. "Don't you have any questions today?"

He shook his head and replied, "I have no questions. The medical camp was the most fulfilling experience of my life. I feel completely satisfied."

Why action works

What changed for Dilip? It wasn't just the work—it was the shift in perspective that comes from serving others. Service pulls us out of our narrow, self-centered mental loops. It grounds us in the present, lending freshness and clarity to the mind.

For a mind consumed by vague problems and endless speculation, *action* provides direction and purpose. It realigns our priorities, helping us discern what truly matters.

The mind thrives on inertia, creating imaginary problems and imaginary solutions in equal measure. Action dismantles this deceptive campaign. It reawakens our energy, shifts our focus outward, and paves the way for real progress.

So, the next time the mind traps you in endless rumination, remember Krishna's advice to Arjuna: "Get up and fight." Turn your thoughts into tangible deeds. When you act with determination and purpose, you'll find that the mind's noise fades, and clarity emerges.

Dealing with confusion about choices

You might say, "I want to take action, but I'm confused about what to do. Should I listen to a class or chant *'Hare Krishna'*? I can't deal with so many choices. I feel stuck in my thoughts. I am overthinking about my *action*!"

When confusion about choices derails you, consider this simple framework:

1. **Is this a good vs. bad choice?**
   If yes, the decision is straightforward—choose the good.
2. **Is this a good vs. good choice?**
   If yes, then toss a coin. Heads for choice A, tails for choice B. Whatever the outcome, just act.

When both choices are inherently positive, thinking is unnecessary because either choice will lead to progress. The mind, however, loves to complicate things.

Why we overthink choices

The mind thrives on control. It whispers that perfection is attainable, that "I need to make the best possible decision to prove my worth." Often, this inaction stems from deeper, subtler causes, such as:

- **Fear**: "What if I fail?"
- **Approval-seeking**: "Will others judge my decision?"
- **Control**: "I want everything to turn out perfectly."
- **Enjoyment**: "Will this be the most pleasurable choice?"
- **Obsession with speed**: "I want results immediately."

These layers create a mental fog, paralyzing us with indecision.

The trap of inertia in action

This dynamic often plays out during the workshops I conduct. When I assign a group or an individual a certain task, some participants hesitate. Their preference for a *satsanga*—a traditional spiritual talk filled with stories, philosophy, and humor—keeps them in their comfort zone. Asking them to engage actively, think critically, or write down their thoughts disrupts their expectations and disturbs their mood.

Their reluctance manifests as seemingly valid questions like, *"How exactly should this be done?"* or *"What if we get it wrong?"* But beneath these inquiries lies a deeper discomfort with stepping out of their habitual patterns.

The same phenomenon happens in my private life. At times, I lie in bed overwhelmed by the thought of "too many things to do." My mind spins excuses like:

- *"Some tasks are impossible right now."*
- *"What if I'm doing the wrong thing first?"*
- *"I need a better plan before starting anything."*

When seen objectively, these excuses are flimsy, manifestations of the mind's inertia and overthinking. Yet in the moment, they seem critically important.

The solution: Kickstart *action*

The key is to recognize overthinking for what it is—a smokescreen for inaction. Left unchecked, this mental fog can lead to unhealthy actions, like:

- Mindlessly scrolling on your phone
- Eating junk food
- Binge-watching a web series

Inaction is still a choice—the choice to avoid positive, meaningful *action*—and it often leads to unhealthy habits.

To counter this, remember: *action* clears confusion. Start with the simplest, most accessible task at hand. Even imperfect action is better than stagnation. Once you begin, the fog lifts, clarity returns, and momentum builds.

When your mind says, "I'm too confused to act," the best response is simple: Ignore it, get up, and do something positive.

#2 A Refreshing New Paradigm of Bhakti-Yoga

Spiritual life is often dismissed as feel-good idealism or abstract emotionalism, especially when it comes to Bhakti-

Yoga. Many perceive it as a path of sentimental love or devotion devoid of tangible value. This misunderstanding can lead some to imagine they are spiritual while neglecting to do anything meaningful or practical in life.

Srila Prabhupada, the great teacher of Bhakti-Yoga, revolutionized this notion with a profound yet pragmatic definition—Bhakti-Yoga *is "devotional service."* Note the emphasis on the word *"service"* in this definition.

Bhakti as practical activity

Srila Prabhupada wrote:

> *"Devotional service is not a matter of sentimental speculation or imaginative ecstasy. Its substance is practical activity... Bhakti is a sort of cultivation. As soon as we say 'cultivation,' we must refer to activity. Cultivation of spirituality does not mean sitting down idly for meditation, as some pseudo-yogīs teach. Such idle meditation may be good for those who have no information of devotional service... The execution of devotional service is not a matter of idle meditation but practical action in the foreground of spiritual life."*
>
> ***(Nectar of Instruction, Verse 3, purport)***

This makes it clear that Bhakti-Yoga is not passive or escapist. It is about engaging in practical, meaningful activities that cultivate a loving connection with God.

Prabhupada often quoted the *Bhagavad Gita* (3.21):

> *"Whatever action is performed by a great man, common men follow in his footsteps. And whatever standards he sets by exemplary acts, all the world pursues."*

Action and remembrance: The twin pillars of Bhakti-Yoga

Bhakti-Yoga combines two essential principles:

1. Action in the form of service.
2. Remembrance of God through love and devotion.

Bhakti-Yoga teachers compare this dual approach to traditional yoga practice. In yoga, one stretches the body while maintaining steady breathing. Similarly, in Bhakti-Yoga, service corresponds to the physical activity of stretching, while remembrance of God is akin to the breathing that sustains the practice. Both are essential to achieve the desired results.

Most spiritual traditions encourage us to approach God for our needs or desires. Srila Prabhupada elevated this understanding. He taught that *true bhakti* means not seeking God for personal fulfillment but serving Him to execute His divine will. As we increase our service and improve our remembrance of God, we'd not turn to God for material blessings; rather we'd seek and find joy in service itself.

Prabhupada's practical example

Once, during a morning walk at his Vrindavan temple, Srila Prabhupada encountered an enthusiastic disciple who loudly exclaimed, *"Srila Prabhupada ki Jai!"* as a gesture of admiration. Srila Prabhupada smiled and continued walking. The disciple repeated this act during the next lap, increasing his enthusiasm each time. On the third round, when the disciple's expression of admiration touched new decibel levels, Srila Prabhupada firmly planted his walking stick on the ground, looked at the disciple, and said:

"Why don't you do something practical and give up this sycophancy? Can you instead clean this veranda?"

This anecdote beautifully illustrates Srila Prabhupada's emphasis on meaningful action over superficial sentimentality. *True bhakti* lies in *practical service,* not hollow displays of devotion.

The power of service

Bhakti-Yoga yields its greatest rewards when approached with a genuine desire to serve. Even if we occasionally fall into overthinking or inertia, the mood of service pulls us back. Service is the preventive medicine for stagnation and the key to progressing on the spiritual path.

When we embody this paradigm of Bhakti-Yoga, we not only align ourselves with divine will but also inspire others to pursue a life of purpose and devotion through our own example.

#3 Hanuman Overcomes Overthinking

It was a race against time. Lord Rama had entrusted Hanuman with a critical mission—to discover the whereabouts of Sita, Rama's consort, who had been abducted by the demon king Ravana. Hanuman, the mighty *Vanara* warrior, had leapt across the vast Indian Ocean to reach Lanka, Ravana's fortress kingdom.

On his way, Hanuman had effortlessly overcome several formidable challenges. He defeated the demoness Simhika, who could capture and devour beings by manipulating their shadows. He grew in size and tore her apart from within.

He also outmaneuvered Lankini, the powerful guardian at Lanka's gates. Now, after infiltrating Ravana's grand palace, Hanuman was frantically searching for Sita. He scoured every chamber, yet she was nowhere to be found.

At this crucial moment, Hanuman felt overwhelmed. Doubts and fears began to cloud his usually sharp mind. *"What if I fail to find her?"*, he thought. This single worry spiraled into a cascade of dreadful scenarios:

- Rama would be heartbroken and might end his life
- Lakshman, ever loyal to his elder brother, would follow suit
- Sugriva, their ally and the leader of the *vanara* army, would succumb to despair and die
- The monkey soldiers, devastated by their king's demise, would also perish
- The people of Ayodhya, already grieving Rama's absence, would be so shattered by the news that they might resort to mass suicide

Hanuman concluded: *All this destruction would be my fault. Perhaps it is better I don't return at all, so at least Lord Rama's hope remains alive. But if I return empty-handed, I would bring him unbearable pain. Shame on me—I am a failure and unworthy of my master's trust!*

Hanuman, the great hero of the *Ramayana*, was now ensnared by the mind's tendency to catastrophize—imagining worst-case scenarios and creating problems that didn't exist. Earlier, during his search of Ravana's chambers, Hanuman had faced another bout of doubt. As he examined the women lying in Ravana's bedroom to check if one of them was

Sita, he suddenly thought: *How can I, a celibate and devout brahmachari, look at these women in such a state? Am I not violating my principles of chastity?*

Hanuman overcame this dilemma by reconnecting with his purpose. He reminded himself that his actions were motivated by service to Lord Rama, and not by personal indulgence. Accepting the situation as a necessary part of his mission, Hanuman focused on his goal and dismissed the distracting thoughts.

Now, feeling despondent at not finding Sita, Hanuman faced a more severe mental battle. But just as before, he found his way out of the quagmire of negative thinking—by taking action. He renewed his resolve and resumed his search with an undiminished vigor.

As the *Ramayana* reveals, Hanuman's perseverance bore fruit. He eventually found Sita in the Ashoka groves, and later delivered the joyous news of her safety to Lord Rama. This discovery became a pivotal moment in the story, leading to Rama's victorious battle against Ravana and the reunion with Sita.

Negative thinking is like a swamp—it can drag down even the strongest of minds. The more you dwell on imagined problems, the deeper you sink. Hanuman's story teaches us that *action* is the cure for overthinking. By reconnecting with your purpose and stepping forward with determination, you can break the mind's illusions and fill yourself with renewed energy and hope.

Action cuts through the fog of doubt and despair, allowing you to see the path forward clearly—just as Hanuman did.

#4 The Logic of Spiritual Action

While action can break the chains of overthinking, it does not necessarily guarantee long-term happiness. Simply being active is not the ultimate goal of life—even animals like birds and monkeys are constantly busy. What truly brings fulfillment is leading a *purpose-centered life*—one where our actions are meaningful, honorable, and add value to others.

Human action operates on three interconnected levels: physical, emotional, and spiritual. Let us examine each and how they influence our sense of drive and satisfaction.

1. Physical action: "I want to enjoy"

Most people act to satisfy their physical needs and desires. Whether it is indulging in delicious food, earning wealth, or pursuing sensory pleasures, the driving force here is the quest for enjoyment.

However, our capacity to enjoy is inherently limited, while our desires are boundless. For instance, the tongue may crave more food than the stomach can handle, and overeating can lead to discomfort and illness. Similarly, the pursuit of material pleasures often comes at a cost.

In this paradigm of "I want to enjoy," actions are motivated by self-gratification. Advertising and media industries amplify this desire, promising happiness through consumption. Yet the more we indulge, the more dissatisfied we often feel. The endless chase for gratification is like pouring fuel on a fire—it only intensifies the craving. Far from bringing peace, this kind of enjoyment often leads to misery.

2. Emotional action: "I want love"

Recognizing the futility of purely physical pleasures, some shift their focus to seeking love and emotional connection. The new paradigm becomes: "I want love."

Love is indeed a fundamental human need, second only to basic survival necessities like food and water. A child nurtured with love grows into an emotionally healthy adult, whereas those deprived of love often spend their lives searching for it.

While love is essential, it, too, has its limitations. Many people receive ample love, yet they continue to feel unloved or incomplete. Emotional fulfillment often mirrors the trap of physical pleasure—the more we get, the more we desire. This endless need for validation, appreciation, and affection can leave us dissatisfied, much like an addiction that never truly satisfies.

3. Spiritual action: "I want to give love"

True contentment arises when we transcend the need to seek pleasure or love and instead focus on giving love.

At our core, we are spiritual beings, and our deepest happiness lies in contributing selflessly to the well-being of others. Unlike the conditional love we often seek, giving love unconditionally is a spiritual act that uplifts both the giver and the recipient.

When we act with the intention to share love, we align with a higher purpose. These spiritual actions create a ripple effect—they bring satisfaction to the body, heart and soul. Paradoxically, when we focus on giving, we also find that our physical and emotional needs are naturally fulfilled.

The paradigm shift: From seeking to giving

When we hear the word *love,* we often imagine receiving it from others. Lasting happiness, however, comes not from receiving, but from giving. Shifting our actions from selfish gratification to contribution transforms not only our experience of life but also the lives of those around us.

Actions rooted in spiritual intent—driven by the desire to give—elevate us beyond the fleeting pleasures of the physical and emotional realms. They bring a sense of inner ease that no material or emotional pursuit can match.

By embracing the mindset of "I want to give love," we unlock a deeper connection to our spiritual nature and experience true fulfillment.

One of my greatest inspirations is my uncle, Mr. Lakshminarayana Acharya, who cleared the prestigious Indian Civil Services exam in the early 1940s. However, inspired by Subhash Chandra Bose and his revolutionary ideals, my uncle made a bold decision: he renounced the prestigious post as a mark of protest against the British Raj.

Determined to meet his inspiration, he sought an audience with Bose, a meeting that profoundly shaped his life. Subhash Chandra Bose advised him to return to his roots and serve his own community. He urged my uncle to empower his town folk by teaching them to read and write and to spread awareness about the cause of India's freedom.

Taking this advice to heart, Mr. Acharya dedicated his life to serving the people of his hometown, Udupi. As a physics professor, he earned enough to support his family, his parents, and seven siblings. Beyond his professional duties, he spent countless hours teaching the underprivileged to read and write, counseling the young and old, and offering his guidance freely. He never sought money or gifts for his services.

Through his actions, Mr. Acharya taught his community the virtues of living with honor and dignity. Although he was honored by his college, town, and even the state government, he sought no recognition, finding fulfillment solely in service and contribution.

These actions, centered on giving love, illuminate the path to true contentment. When one is deeply engaged in such meaningful service, overthinking becomes a distant, irrelevant concern.

#5 A Life of Service

In my monastery, I witness monks who serve tirelessly and happily, seven days a week, for 10 to 12 hours each day. Their lives are driven by a strong sense of purpose and a desire to give.

One such monk, my friend Manohar, who hails from a small town near Pune, Maharashtra, embodies this spirit of service. For over 26 years, I have watched him dedicate himself to the needs of the ashram—cleaning the sacred altar, maintaining the temple premises, mentoring younger monks, and cooking for the community.

When I mentioned to him that I was writing a book on overthinking, he seemed amused. "Oh, is overthinking really that big a problem in society?" he asked with genuine curiosity. After I explained its ubiquitous presence in society, his response was characteristic of him: he joined his palms, looked upward in silent prayer for those suffering, and excused himself to continue his service.

Manohar has no time for gossip or lamenting about situations he cannot change. Instead, he focuses his energy on being part of the solution—a vital cog in humanity's effort to serve and bring light to the world.

Manohar is just one of over a hundred monks in our ashram. Across ISKCON and other spiritual organizations, countless men and women lead lives of meaningful service, transcending the mind's tendency to exaggerate and inflate trivial issues.

#6 Srila Prabhupada's Wisdom on Overthinking – Action more Important than Feelings

Srila Prabhupada often illustrated the futility of overthinking through the story of an old woman who worried incessantly about an upcoming fair in her village.

As the day of the fair approached, she fretted, "How will the crowds be accommodated? Where will they eat? How will the fair be organized? What if something goes wrong?" She panicked so much that her family couldn't console her.

The fair came and went without any incident. The sun rose the next morning, life resumed as usual, and her fears proved baseless. So, as Srila Prabhupada explained, she had wasted precious time and energy worrying about things beyond her control.

Srila Prabhupada's advice is both devotional and practical: focus on what you can realistically do to be part of the solution rather than get mournful over what you cannot change. He often encouraged his students to chant *Hare Krishna*, study scriptures, and engage in other practices of Bhakti-Yoga—even when they didn't feel particularly inspired. *Bhakti*, he emphasized, is rooted in practical action and service, not fleeting emotions. Feelings, as he often reminded us, are transient. Due to the fickle nature of the mind, good feelings will come and go, but it is the discipline that brings lasting rewards.

I recently experienced the transformative power of Srila Prabhupada's advice to prioritize practical action over overthinking. One morning, I was scheduled to write in my scripture journal. (We'll delve into this type of journaling and its benefits in Chapter 4 of this book.) As I sat at my desk, notebook open, I felt an overwhelming lethargy creep in. I simply didn't feel like writing. I knew I needed to act, yet my mind resisted. Inspiration was absent.

Having spoken many times in my classes about the need to move from *motivated feelings* to *disciplined actions* for success in any endeavor, I was now confronted with the challenge of applying that principle. From past experience, I knew motivation is temporary and fades over time, while discipline grows stronger with consistency and ultimately helps us achieve our goals. Yet, in that moment, my knowledge felt futile as my mind refused to cooperate.

I paused, took a deep breath, and practiced *awareness and acceptance*. I noticed the chatter in my mind. Chanchal was quick to offer excuses: *"What's the point of writing today?" "You have written thousands of pages; missing one won't matter." "There is a delicious breakfast waiting—upma and rasam. Eat first, then write." "There is nothing worth writing about this topic anyway."*

Instead of arguing with Chanchal, I simply observed its chatter without judgment. I accepted each excuse as it came, repeating to myself with a breath, *"It's okay, just breathe."* Gradually, the voice began to fade. Seizing the moment, I mustered all my willpower, picked up my pen, and started writing.

What happened next surprised me. Just two minutes into writing, ideas began to flow effortlessly. Connections between different chapters of the scriptures became clear, and realizations emerged. I discovered a depth of understanding about a particular section of the *Bhagavad Gita* that I hadn't recognized before. For the next forty minutes, I wrote with inspiration and clarity. The resulting essay not only amazed me but was also well-received when I later shared it with my audience.

That morning, I felt grateful for not letting my overthinking mind hijack my higher self. I also realized a crucial truth: one of the mind's greatest obstacles to effective action is its overemphasis on *motivation* rather than *discipline.* True progress comes from showing up and acting, even when the feelings aren't there.

Balancing thought and action

While some—like the old woman in the story above—overthink without taking action, others act impulsively without introspection. Both approaches can lead to frustration. Overthinking immobilizes us, while unreflective action can be misled by unhealthy desires of the mind or driven by hatred.

The key lies in balanced action—mindfully engaging in activities that align with purpose and values. By focusing on service and contribution, we can transcend the mind's trap and lead lives of true contentedness.

#7 The Tragedy of Harmful Action

The world held its breath as the greatest race in history unfolded. The scene was set at the 1988 Seoul Olympics, where American track and field athlete Carl Lewis, the celebrated Olympic champion, faced off against the sensational Canadian sprinter Ben Johnson, who held the world record and was chasing his first Olympic gold.

In the previous Olympics, Lewis had won four gold medals but had become unpopular due to his perceived lack of humility. When Johnson shattered the world record two years later and defeated Lewis for the first time, Lewis responded cynically alleging that Johnson's performance was drug-enhanced. Thus began one of the most infamous rivalries in sports history.

The Seoul 100m final lasted less than 10 seconds, but its impact was seismic. Johnson's astonishing 9.79-second finish broke his own previous record and earned him a hero's welcome back home. Canada celebrated, with its prime minister calling to congratulate him. The world marveled at Johnson's seemingly superhuman achievement, coining terms like "Benfastic" to describe his feat.

However, within a day, the glory crumbled. Johnson failed a doping test and his gold medal was rewarded to Lewis, who had finished second. The banner headlines were merciless: "Hero to Zero in 9.79 seconds."

Determined to make a comeback, Johnson won a 50m race in France five years later, only to fail another doping test. This time, he was banned for life. His downfall was a bitter pill for athletics fans.

The fallout of harmful action

The "dirtiest race in history" as the Seoul final came to be called, left an indelible stain on athletics. Lewis, who inherited the gold medal, was not without controversy. Footage from the race revealed he had run out of his lane twice, which should have led to automatic disqualification. Moreover, it emerged later that Lewis had tested positive during trials before the Olympics. Even Linford Christie, the silver medallist, was banned for steroid use a decade later.

Amidst this chaos, the true hero of the race went unnoticed: Calvin Smith, the unassuming bronze medallist. Smith, a clean athlete who had never been implicated in doping scandals throughout his career, was overshadowed by the drama surrounding his rivals. His quiet integrity was a stark contrast to the tainted glory of others, yet history barely remembers him.

As Shakespeare poignantly noted in *Julius Caesar*, "The evil that men do lives after them, while the good is oft buried with their bones." Calvin Smith's legacy reminds us of another Shakespearean truth: "No legacy is as rich as honesty."

Competing with others vs. Competing with ourselves

What is more important for an athlete—or for any of us: to compete against others or to measure ourselves against our own conscience? When we obsess over rivals, we lose sight of our true purpose. The greatest accountability we have is to our inner self. Action without introspection can be harmful, just as introspection without action can lead to overthinking and delusion.

In his autobiography, *From Seoul to Soul*, one might expect Ben Johnson to reflect on his mistakes. Sadly, the book focuses on attacking Carl Lewis, even making bizarre claims about their rivalry extending back to a supposed past life in ancient Egypt. Such thinking underscores the dangers of unexamined action and unresolved bitterness.

A higher purpose

Environmentalist David Brower once said, "We don't inherit the earth from our ancestors; we borrow it from our children." His words remind us that our actions must transcend personal gain and contribute to a legacy of goodness. Whether in athletics or in life, what truly matters is not the glamor of fleeting success but the impact we leave on others.

True champions are not defined by medals but by the light they bring into the world. To achieve this, our actions must be rooted in spiritual awareness. The essence of such action is embodied in the desire to give love—to serve others and uplift humanity.

The life of Hanuman, the great servant of the *Ramayana*, exemplifies this spirit. Hanuman played an indispensable role in Lord Rama's victory over Ravana, yet in the *Mahabharata*, he willingly assumed a humble position, sitting atop Arjuna's chariot and roaring in encouragement. In our world, it is akin to a cricket player winning the "Man of the Series" award in one tournament and serving as the twelfth man in the next. Hanuman, however, was content in service rather than recognition.

To overcome harmful action, we must first address the damaging thoughts that fuel it. In the final chapter of this book, we will explore how wisdom literature and spiritual practices can guide us to perform actions that align with our best interests and highest aspirations. True happiness comes not from fleeting achievements but from living with integrity, humility, and a commitment to serve. This is the legacy of real champions.

#8 Thinking – Experience Dynamics

Overthinking can destabilize our minds, and harmful actions only exacerbate the situation. When overthinking overwhelms us, some may react by indulging in destructive behaviors like angry outbursts, consuming alcohol or drugs, binge-eating, or immersing themselves in a stimulating web series to distract their minds. This behavior provides a pain-killer effect—a fleeting sense of relief when we vent our frustrations or numb ourselves, but soon, the pain returns with even more intensity. The cycle repeats: cravings for more food, endless scrolling through reels, and watching shows on OTT platforms. At the end of it all, we have probably moved further away from where we wanted to be. Overthinking can, therefore, seamlessly lead us to actions that betray our own values.

To prevent this downward spiral, it is crucial to remember: "Thinking is vastly different from experience."

I may spend two precious hours in the morning planning my week and still remain indecisive about what to do and why. In doing so, I have missed out on a hundred minutes of beautiful experiences that the early hours of the day could have offered me.

Almost all action is an attempt to gain a positive experience, but when experience is lacking, we tend to overthink or seek stimulation, which only takes us further away from the genuine experiences we long for.

In our minds, we often oscillate between imagining pleasures or dwelling on problems that need solving. In doing so, we deny ourselves peace. Our inner world contains three houses: sense gratification or stimulation (pleasure), struggle (problem-solving), and shelter or satisfaction (peace). Overthinking is a prime example of living in the struggle zone—we go around in circles, worrying aimlessly without tangible solutions or actions. The harder we think, the more elusive the answers become. It is like the proverbial child chasing a ball in a river, or a donkey chasing a carrot dangling just out of reach.

Seeking stimulation vs. The path to satisfaction

In addition to the elusive solution, our sedentary response to overthinking only compounds our problems. We want to feel in control of our lives, but fail to realize that it is precisely our overthinking that denies us that control. We need to let go and surrender.

When we release the desire to control, recognizing that thinking gives us only an illusion of control, and instead surrender to the present moment, we open the door to positive experiences. This requires trust in a force beyond ourselves. We must practice patience and engage in persistent, meaningful action. Unfortunately, we are often lured by the cheaper alternative—stimulation. Munching on potato chips or binge-watching mundane shows provides a quick fix of dopamine, temporarily numbing our overthinking mind.

However, these fleeting distractions only leave our hearts feeling empty, driving us to seek relief from the worry that plagues us. In the process, we deny ourselves the opportunity to access deeper, more fulfilling satisfaction.

Satisfaction and stimulation are like chalk and cheese—completely different. Watching a sunrise outside your window satisfies the heart, while watching the same sunrise on your electronic screen merely stimulates you.

Take a moment to assess your choices: How often do you opt for stimulation rather than true satisfaction?

Stimulation offers temporary relief, helping us move from a negative state (let's say, -5) to neutral (0). Satisfaction, on the other hand, takes us from neutral to a positive state (5).

The logical question that arises is: How do we move from overthinking and stimulation to satisfaction and positive experiences?

As we let go of the desire to control and connect to the present moment, cultivating the desire to give love, we unlock spiritual experiences that are far more fulfilling. To give love or service is our constitutional position, and that alone brings satisfaction. Just as water is liquid in its original state, salt is salty, and sugar is sweet, we, too, are naturally inclined toward service. As pure souls, part and parcel of the divine, our essence is rooted in service.

When we shift our paradigm from seeking pleasure to giving love, we access a deeper aspect of our existence. This conscious, deliberate shift toward a life of service—the platform of the soul—helps us reconnect with our true identity. In living and acting with the intention to serve, we access the true happiness that we long for.

#9 Our Real Identity – The Foundation of Meaningful Action

When we make the paradigm shift—from *"I want pleasure"* or *"I want love"* to *"I want to give love"*—we also connect with our true self, the *"I"* that exists beyond the overthinking and problems of this world.

Srila Prabhupada often used a simple analogy to illustrate how we are not the bodies we inhabit. Just as a driver is distinct from the car they drive, we, as individuals, are not our bodies, minds, or egos. I am a pure spirit soul, separate from the body I currently occupy. Through practices like service, meditation, and gratitude, we can access our real self—the true *"I"*.

The foundation of spiritually fulfilling action is rooted in the understanding that "I am not the body; I am a spirit soul." The more we embrace this truth and live from the perspective of the soul, the more overthinking gives way to positive, purposeful action.

Understanding what we are not

To access our real, spiritual identity, we first need to understand what we are not.

We often think and act according to the false identity of our body and mind, which leads us into confusion and distraction. The *Taittiriya Upanishad*, a section of the *Yajurveda*, describes the five sheaths that obscure our true identity. These sheaths represent layers of illusion that prevent us from recognizing our pure, spiritual nature. By gradually shedding these layers, we can uncover our essence and live in alignment with our true self.

#10 The Five Sheaths That Cover the Soul

The food body – *Annamaya kosha*

When your head aches, you might say, "I have a headache." However, the truth is that it is not *you* who is experiencing the headache—it is your body. This is the *annamaya kosha*, or the sheath of the physical body. The word "*anna*" refers to food or the body and "*maya*" means made of, while "*kosha*" means sheath. You identify so deeply with your body that you mistakenly say, "I am having a headache," when, in reality, it is your body that is in discomfort. Similarly, when you say, "I am getting old," it is your body that is aging, not *you*—the eternal soul within this body. The *annamaya kosha* is the outermost covering, the visible flesh and mass of the body, with which we strongly identify.

The life force – *Pranamaya kosha*

The second covering is the *pranamaya kosha*, which refers to the life force or "*prana*." This vital energy flows through the body, even though we cannot see it directly. It is responsible for processes like blood circulation, energy conversion from food, and oxygen absorption in the blood. *Prana* helps maintain our bodily functions, and we experience its presence through sensations like hunger, health, fatigue, and energy. When you say, "I am tired" or "I am hungry," it is, again, your identification with the life force—the *pranamaya kosha*—not your true self.

Upon closer observation, we notice that both our body and life force constantly change but the real *"I"* remains unchanged. As a child, I was small and now I am an adult; my body has transformed. At times, I feel energetic, and other times I have no appetite. These fluctuations occur in the *pranamaya kosha*, but the *real self*, the observing subject, remains constant.

The mind sheath – *Manomaya kosha*

When you say, "I am sad" or "I am angry," it is important to recognize that it is not the true *you* experiencing these emotions—it is your mind. The *manomaya kosha* is the mental sheath that governs thoughts, feelings, and emotions. Many people mistakenly identify themselves with their emotions, but they are not their minds. The mind is subtler than the body and the life force, yet it remains an object of experience, while *you*, the soul, are the subject.

You can separate yourself from your mind in the same way you would separate your hand from your body by saying, "This is my hand." Similarly, you can say, "These are my thoughts" or "These are my desires," but you are not these thoughts or desires. You are the observer of them, not the thoughts themselves.

The intellect - *Vijnanamaya kosha*

When you are unable to make a decision and say, "I am confused," it is not *you* who is confused; it is your intellect that lacks clarity. The *vijnanamaya kosha* refers to the intellect, which is subtler than the body, life force, and mind. Yet it is still an object of experience, not the true self. When you say, "I understand" or "I don't understand," you are referring to the functioning of your intellect. However, you are not the intellect; it, too, is a changing object.

Your intellect, like your mind, has the ability to learn and forget. For example, there was a time when you didn't know the periodic table or that tan theta is equal to sin theta by cos theta. Then you went to high school and learnt chemistry and trigonometry and now four decades later, you may have forgotten the periodic table. You are the same person who remembers and forgets. Intellect, therefore, is also a changing object and you are the unchanging witness of your intellect.

The *vijnanamaya kosha* is also a changing object, and you are its unchanging witness.

The bliss body - *Anandamaya kosha*

The *anandamaya kosha* is the closest covering to our true self. When you experience deep happiness or contentment, such as when you enjoy a chocolate ice cream, you become so absorbed in the experience that you temporarily forget your body and mind. This is the bliss body—the experience of *ananda*, or bliss. In deep sleep, when your intellect is inactive, you wake up feeling refreshed and declare that you experienced deep peace, as you were unaware of your surroundings.

Though this may seem to be closest to our true self, it still isn't. The fact that you are able to declare that you were unaware during sleep means that you are separate from the experience of bliss. This "not knowing" is itself a form of knowing. The question arises: Who was it that experienced the absence of thought or the total shutdown of the intellect during deep sleep or moments of intense bliss? The true *"I"* is beyond even this bliss body.

In summary, each of the five sheaths—the *annamaya kosha* (food body), *pranamaya kosha* (life force), *manomaya kosha* (mind), *vijnanamaya kosha* (intellect), and *anandamaya kosha* (bliss body)—are all layers that obscure our true, spiritual identity. As we progress in self-awareness, we move closer to understanding that we are the unchanging soul, distinct from these temporary coverings.

#11 Blending the *Pancha Koshas* and Three A's to Cure Overthinking

The soul, or the true self, is covered by five layers or sheaths—the *pancha koshas.* By merging the understanding of these sheaths with the tools of *awareness, acceptance, and action* (the three A's), we can move beyond our material, bodily identity and return to a state of recognizing our true, spiritual essence.

Imagine you have been overthinking about a recurring back pain, and an MRI report reveals a dark patch. A few days later, you have an appointment with a specialist who might diagnose you with cancer. The thought of this possibility starts eating away at you.

You can address the debilitating effects of overthinking by first practicing *awareness*:

"My mind is thinking that I might have cancer. My *manomaya kosha* (mind sheath) is fearful, anxious, and restless. I am a pure spirit soul, different from this anxious mind. Yet, due to my misidentification with the mind's worries, I feel disconnected from reality. I am also aware that my intellect (*vijnanamaya kosha*) lacks clarity and is confused about my situation. Furthermore, my body (*annamaya kosha*) is in pain, and because of my constant worry, my breathing has become shallow. Hence, my *pranamaya kosha* (life force) is disturbed."

This step helps you separate yourself from the mind's barrage of thoughts and recognize that the suffering is happening in your five sheaths, not in your true self. By practicing *awareness*, you successfully disidentify from the suffering caused by overthinking.

At first, you might find this process challenging and superficial, especially if you are unfamiliar with the practice of the three A's. However, with practice, you'll find that you can puncture overthinking much faster.

Next, comes *acceptance*:

"I accept that my body, life force, mind, and intellect are in disarray. I accept that I need to commit to a daily routine of back exercises to help manage the pain. I will pause now, take a deep breath, and slowly inhale and exhale to restore balance to my *pranamaya kosha*. To calm my mind, I affirm that I am safe and healthy."

Acceptance involves acknowledging the imbalances in your sheaths and slowly deciding to take action for self-care.

This approach is a form of positive thinking, shifting you from the debilitating "Why?" mindset to the empowering "What?" mindset. Instead of asking, "Why me?" or "Why has this happened to me?"—which only intensifies overthinking—*awareness* and *acceptance* help you focus on actionable steps like, "What can I do to improve my health?" or "What is the next step to bring peace to my mind?"

The first two steps help you shift your mindset from one of fear and uncertainty to that of hope and possibility.

That's when you move to the third A—*action*:

Now you take decisive steps—picking up the phone not to mindlessly scroll through social media, but to call a friend. You grab your paper and pen and write down your thoughts in a journal. By taking *action*, you rupture the cycle of overthinking and regain control of your mind.

Each time overthinking pulls you down, you can return to the three A's.

You might be thinking: "But when I'm caught in overthinking, I can't remember the three A's. It feels like more of a cognitive exercise, and that's precisely what I lack in those moments. When I'm overthinking, my mind feels overwhelmed, and I don't have the bandwidth to apply a mental tool."

If this is your concern, you need to incorporate a second device: *breathing*.

Turn to the next chapter to discover the art of breathing and relaxation, which will help you calm the mind and create space for the three A's to work.

Part B

Breathe

CHAPTER 2

Breathe

"Lord Krishna said, "O mighty-armed son of Kunti, it is undoubtedly very difficult to curb the restless mind, but it is possible by suitable practice and by detachment."

—*The Bhagavad Gita* (6.36)

Paum! The engine howled, its thunderous roar reverberating through the air as the train's gaping mouth loomed closer, threatening to crush my very existence. I stood mere centimetres away from a speeding train. My heart was pounding in sync with the metallic clatter of wheels against rails. My reckless decision to save time by crossing the tracks, glancing only at the empty platform and ignoring the possibility of an approaching train, had brought me to this perilous moment.

It was a routine morning when I was on my way to the university. My headphones blaring loud Bollywood music, I was oblivious to the world. I faintly registered the distant honking of an engine. Turning my head, I was greeted by the terrifying sight of death charging toward me at full speed. The realization hit like a lightning bolt—my time was running out.

Without a second to think, I acted on instinct. Planting my hands on the platform edge, I propelled myself away from the tracks. The train rushed past, brushing my shirt, its deafening roar filling the air. I lay sprawled on the platform, saved by a whisker. Around me, the station stood frozen, passengers wide-eyed and aghast at my reckless feat.

As I staggered to my feet, still trembling from the brush with death, shame flooded me. I avoided the stares of the men and women who gawked at me, their expressions a mix of disbelief and disdain. Before I could process what had just transpired, an elderly man stormed toward me. Without warning, he delivered a sharp slap across my cheek.

"Are you out of your mind?" he thundered, his voice trembling with anger and concern. "You think you're Shahrukh Khan pulling stunts for the movies? If you're so desperate to risk your life, join the army and fight at the border! At least you'd die doing something worthwhile for the country."

His words stung more than the slap, and I stood there, stunned and chastened. In that moment, the weight of my stupidity crashed over me. I had gambled with my life for no reason at all, and the cost could have been irreparable.

At twenty-two, I was brazen and invincible—or so I thought. That illusion shattered after my close brush with death. Sitting on a bench at the platform, my chest heaved with rapid, fearful breaths as disdainful glances from onlookers bore into me. Though I tried to regain composure, the shock refused to subside. Instead of catching a train to college, I turned back and went home, shaken to my core.

For the next week, I barely stepped out of my room. My heart raced incessantly, my body trembled, and every attempt at distraction failed. Nightmares replayed the incident relentlessly, each one more vivid than the last. I couldn't bring myself to share the story with anyone, burdened by fear and shame.

Now, thirty-two years later, when the memory resurfaces, an inexplicable fear grips me. My breathing quickens, my head spins, and my body jolts into a fight-or-flight state. It is as if I have become a hen—pecking at the ground for worms while constantly scanning for the lurking shadow of a predator ready to strike. My sympathetic nervous system kicks into overdrive, leaving me jittery and shallow-breathed. Three decades later, my mind is still terrorized by what could have happened.

This reaction isn't unique to me. We all have close calls in life, and while the immediate danger passes, the fear often lingers. Even when no visible threats remain, our minds stay locked in battle, replaying scenarios, keeping us perpetually on edge. Like that fearful hen, we live in a constant state of suspicion and defense, guarding our body, mind, and ego from imaginary enemies.

The more we live in this battle-ready state, the shallower our breathing becomes—a vicious cycle with devastating effects. Shallow breathing feeds fear, insecurity, and a scarcity mindset, catabolically wearing down our psyche and body. The world feels hostile and unsafe because our inner state mirrors that tension.

Conversely, the key to breaking this cycle lies in the breath itself. By consciously working on our breath—slowing it down, deepening it—we create space for safety and calm. The mind follows suit, slowing its anxious chatter. This shift has an anabolic effect on our tissues, fostering healing, clarity, and a sense of abundance.

Breath is more than life; it is a gateway to peace. When we take control of it, we reclaim our inner world from fear and scarcity, transforming it into a sanctuary of strength and security.

I can't help contrasting the reckless train incident with a spiritual experience that I had around the same time.

Both events left lasting impressions on me, but they shaped my inner world in profoundly different ways.

Around that period, I had begun practicing *Hare Krishna* meditation and occasionally visited the local ISKCON temple. It had been six months since I was introduced to the science and techniques of chanting *Hare Krishna*, and I found myself drawn to the temple, especially on weekends. Among the various preachers and monks, His Holiness Radhanath Swami stood out. His talks were simple yet deeply heart-touching. He presented God not as an abstract entity but as Krishna, the Supreme Personality of Godhead—a personal, loving figure.

What intrigued me most was Radhanath Swami's journey. Born Richard Slavin, a Jewish American, he had left the comforts of his Chicago home as a teenager in search of spiritual fulfillment. By divine providence, he was guided to Srila Prabhupada and Lord Krishna, who captured his heart. He joined as a full-time monk in 1972 and, since 1986, had been a spiritual guide and leader of the Mumbai ISKCON community, inspiring thousands of devotees and monks with his wisdom and example.

One quiet afternoon in the summer of 1998, I was alone in the temple hall, chanting my *japa* on my beads. The temple was serene, with a hushed stillness that amplified the sacred atmosphere. Suddenly, I felt a gentle hand on my shoulder. Startled, I opened my eyes and looked up to see Radhanath Swami standing before me, smiling warmly. Overcome with a mix of surprise and reverence, I immediately stood up and offered my respectful *pranam* with folded palms.

He asked how I was doing, and we spoke for a while. I was astonished—how did he know me? Among the thousand men and women who attended his classes, I was just another face in the crowd. True, I sat at the front, soaking in every word of his discourses, but it was a pleasant and humbling surprise that he recognized and acknowledged me. As I shared some of the insights I had gained from his talks, he listened intently, his gentle demeanor making me feel truly heard. When I finished, he smiled again and complimented me on my sincerity and attentiveness in my spiritual practices.

As he prepared to leave for a meeting, he spread his arms and embraced me. In that moment, tears began to stream down my face. I felt an overwhelming surge of happiness and love flood my heart. It was as if a long-held tension had finally melted away. I exhaled deeply—a breath of profound relief—and felt as though I had come home. A sense of safety and belonging enveloped me, ineffable yet undeniably real. Tears continued to flow as my heart expanded in gratitude and joy.

Even today, twenty-six years later, the memory of that exchange brings me peace. Whenever I recall it, my mind slows down, my heart opens, and my body instinctively relaxes. My breath becomes slow and deep, and a warm feeling of being loved fills my consciousness.

#1 The Logic of Conscious Breathing

Love and fear are contrasting emotional experiences, and they elicit opposite physical reactions in the body. Love fosters relaxation and encourages slow, natural breathing, while fear triggers a defensive, fight-or-flight response that disturbs breathing patterns. These physiological responses are not just temporary; over time, they shape our mental state.

Reflecting on my own experiences—a *deathly scare* like my train incident, and a *loving embrace* like my guru's blessing—I have observed how these moments influenced my inner world. Though the immediate reactions differ, both have the potential to leave lasting imprints on our subconscious. Over time, we can become conditioned to one of these states as our brain's default setting: either living in fear or in a state of love.

When fear dominates, our breathing becomes rapid and shallow, reinforcing feelings of anxiety and insecurity. In contrast, love induces slow, deep breathing, bringing relaxation and a sense of safety. Here lies the secret: if we consciously regulate our breathing—slowing it down and deepening it—we can shift from a state of fear to one of love.

Some spiritually evolved individuals seem to dwell perpetually in love and peace, as though they feel the continuous embrace of the Divine. Their presence is calming, and anyone entering their energy field feels that peace radiating outward. I vividly remember my first encounter with Radhanath Swami. Hours after our brief interaction, I remained in an emotional high, my heart brimming with joy. If I felt so much love from his momentary touch, I marveled at how much love and happiness he must carry in his heart to share so effortlessly.

Contrast this with individuals trapped in fear and anxiety. Their inner world is chaotic, their breathing erratic. They live as though constantly facing a speeding train, haunted by pain and distress from past traumas. Even years after the triggering events, their minds replay those experiences, keeping them in a perpetual state of fear. This internal turmoil manifests physically—fluctuating heart rates, abnormal blood pressure, and chronic agitation. Being around such individuals often leaves others feeling drained and restless.

So, let me ask: when was the last time you truly relaxed and exhaled slowly, basking in love? Conversely, how often in a single day do you catch yourself inhaling rapidly, gripped by fear?

Just as love and fear influence our breathing, we can reverse-engineer this process. By consciously adjusting our breathing—slowing it down and focusing on exhalation—we can reverse fearful memories and invoke positive emotions. This simple practice not only improves emotional well-being but also enhances physical health, creating a harmonious state for body and spirit.

Over the last five years, I have experienced the transformative power of conscious, silent breathing. It has helped me transition from an overthinking, anxious state to a more peaceful and centered mental space. In the following sections, I will share one of the techniques I have practiced that significantly changed my relationship with my mind and breath.

#2 'Eleven into Three' – A Simple Breathing Technique

Five years ago, I began struggling with a recurring problem during my nights: I'd wake up at midnight to use the washroom, but when I returned to bed, sleep eluded me. My mind would race, bouncing from one issue to another. The harder I tried to relax, the more restless I became. This nightly frustration began taking a toll on my daily life—I was irritable, fatigued, and less effective in my work and service.

One particular night was especially harrowing. I dreamt that my best friend had been murdered amidst riots, fire, and gunfire. The vivid nightmare startled me awake and left me drenched in sweat. I got up, used the washroom, and returned to bed, desperate to calm down. But as soon as I closed my eyes, the nightmare resumed exactly where it had left off, as though I were re-watching the same horrific scene in a movie theater after an intermission.

I woke up again, shocked and confused. My mind spiraled into overthinking: *Why is this happening? Did I interact with negative people? Did I eat something wrong?* The more I pondered, the further I drifted from sleep, and my inner turmoil deepened.

It was then that I remembered a simple breathing technique I had learned but never fully utilized for myself. I decided to give it a try.

Here is what I did:

1. **Slow breathing with counting:** I inhaled to a count of four, held my breath for a moment, and exhaled slowly

to the same count. After the exhale, I mentally said the number "one" to keep track.

2. **Repeat and reset:** I continued this process—inhale, hold, exhale, count—until I reached "eleven." When I reached eleven, I declared to myself, "Round one over; I now start round two." I began again from "one," aiming to complete three such rounds.

As I progressed, my mind began wandering back to my worries. When I realized this, I gently brought my focus back to my breath and the count. By the middle of the third round, I drifted off into a deep, restful sleep.

The next morning, I woke up feeling rejuvenated. It was remarkable, but I wasn't entirely sure if this was a one-time fluke. However, the following night confirmed it wasn't. When I again woke up in the middle of the night, I repeated the "eleven into three" technique. This time, I fell asleep midway through the second round.

This simple breathing practice soon became my go-to solution for insomnia. Not only did it help me fall asleep effortlessly, but it also altered the quality of my dreams—they became calmer and more pleasant.

Why it works

The magic of this technique lies in its ability to regulate breathing, quieten the mind, and create a meditative state conducive to sleep. When you consciously focus on slow, measured breaths, your body shifts from the stress-induced "fight or flight" mode to the "rest and digest" state of the parasympathetic nervous system. Counting serves as an anchor, preventing your mind from wandering into anxious or racing thoughts.

Beyond sleep

Occasionally, there were nights when, even after three rounds of breathing, sleep didn't come. Instead of feeling frustrated, I realized that my body was simply signaling that I was already well-rested. On such nights, I would lie in bed and continue breathing slowly, observing how calm and peaceful my mind had become. Even without additional sleep, I felt more rejuvenated and productive during the day because of the mental clarity and relaxation achieved through this practice.

The "eleven into three" breathing technique became a transformative tool for me—not only for combating insomnia but also for fostering a peaceful mental state. It taught me the connection between breath and well-being, a lesson I carry with me every day.

It is a simple psychological trick. When we count from one to eleven while breathing slowly, we create a powerful bridge to mindfulness. Without this focus, our mind often drifts, and our breathing once again becomes shallow and unconscious. The essence of breath management lies in cultivating awareness of the gentle rhythm of inhaling and exhaling. This conscious breathing soothes the overthinking, restless mind. However, maintaining such awareness is challenging when the mind is preoccupied. Counting numbers helps anchor the mind to the present moment, enabling us to reconnect with our breath. The deeper this connection becomes, the more peaceful the mind feels.

I have often noticed that as soon as I start consciously breathing, I become aware of how stiff my body feels. It is like standing in front of a speeding train. Without that pause to breathe consciously, I wouldn't even realize I'm stuck in 'fight or flight' mode. The more I focus on my breath, the more I can let go and relax.

Over time, with regular breathing breaks, I have found it becomes second nature. Just as I instinctively grab a glass of water when I'm thirsty, I now naturally turn to conscious breathing when I feel tired or stressed. It is like responding to a full bladder—you take a bathroom break. Similarly, when your mind feels overloaded, you take a breathing break.

#3 Why Breathing Consciously Matters

In the 1920s, scientists discovered neurons—nerve cells in the brain that communicate through electrical signals. These signals create *brain waves*, rhythmic electrical patterns measurable in Hertz (Hz). The frequency of these waves reflects our mental state, ranging from high activity to deep relaxation.

- **Beta waves (15–40 Hz):**
  When we breathe unconsciously and live busy, fast-paced lives, our brain operates at a high beta frequency. This state supports alertness and activity but, in excess, correlates with stress and anxiety.
- **Alpha waves (7–14 Hz):**
  A relaxed but focused brain functions operates at alpha frequency. This state blends calmness with mental clarity,

fostering creativity and balanced attention. Interestingly, alpha waves are often linked to intuitive insights. For example, you may search tirelessly for a misplaced item like an umbrella, only to give up in frustration. Days later, while relaxing on the couch, the solution suddenly surfaces—it was behind the refrigerator all along. This "aha" moment often occurs when the brain is in a relaxed alpha state.

- **Theta waves (4–7 Hz):**
  Deeper relaxation or light meditation slows the brain further into theta frequency. In this state, we access intuition, creativity, and subconscious insights.
- **Delta waves (0.5–4 Hz):**
  These low-frequency waves dominate during deep sleep and lucid dreams, and are essential for physical healing, regeneration, and spiritual connection.

Slow, intentional breathing directly influences brain wave activity, shifting us from high-frequency beta waves to the calmer alpha or theta states. This transition not only alleviates stress but also enhances focus, creativity, and emotional stability.

By counting while breathing, you redirect your mind from distractions to the present, creating a calming feedback loop. This simple practice not only quietens the mind but also nurtures a healthier, more effective brain. You could then navigate life's challenges with clarity and resilience.

#4 Relaxation – A Swear Word?

"He who is regulated in his habits of eating, sleeping, recreation, and work can mitigate all material pains by practicing the yoga system."

—*The Bhagavad Gita* (6.17)

I once conducted a seminar on "relaxation" for twenty-five leaders from one of our communities. From the outset, I sensed discomfort among the participants. Many of them had never attended a workshop that emphasized rest and taking breaks. The uneasiness finally came to a head when one of the senior leaders blurted out, "If we highlight relaxation, our members might end up eating pizza and sleeping all day. How would we run our organization or community? Do you realize what's at stake?"

His challenge hung in the air, and I could feel the nervous gazes of the others. I replied, "Do you hear me suggesting that we need to relax and rest all the time? Is lethargy and irresponsibility the message I'm delivering?"

My counter-question caught him off guard. "Hmm, no, I don't hear you saying that, but..."

I interrupted gently, "But you're afraid our leaders might misunderstand and misuse this emphasis on relaxation?"

"Yeah, that's my fear," he admitted candidly.

"The difference between you and me," I said calmly, "might be that I trust these leaders to balance relaxation with their responsibilities. What about you? Do you trust them?"

"I guess so," he said, hesitantly. "But something still doesn't feel right."

Turning to the rest of the group, I asked, "What about you all? What's causing this reluctance?"

The room fell quiet as participants exchanged uncertain glances. Then, one member broke the silence: "I think 'relax' is a swear word in our community."

The room erupted in laughter, even the challenger smiled wryly.

The senior leader who had raised the concern sighed deeply. "Our community is built on selfless service and dedication. We push ourselves hard to manage countless services and projects. But, honestly, we have stretched ourselves too thin. Stress is increasing, and members are burning out."

Another participant echoed his sentiments, explaining how a few leaders bore the brunt of responsibilities while many of the 3,000-plus community members remained complacent or disinterested in congregation and temple affairs. Others chimed in, pointing to issues of poor planning, disorganization, and an inability to set boundaries.

One woman summed it up thoughtfully: "We're so busy helping others, we have forgotten to take care of ourselves."

The discussion, which started with skepticism, had evolved into a cathartic exchange of frustrations.

"What can we do to help ourselves?" I asked.

The answers came quickly: "Declutter," "Take time off," "Learn to say no," and "Ask for help."

As their ideas settled, I posed a seemingly unrelated question: "When you breathe normally, what happens to your stomach? Does it go in when you inhale or does it go out?"

"In!" some voices said confidently.

"Out!" others countered.

The twenty-five men and women spontaneously burst into laughter as they realized they weren't sure about one of the most basic human functions.

Curious, I pursued the debate. Some staunchly defended their stance of "In," while others argued for "Out."

"We are humans, supposedly the most evolved species," I quipped with a smile, "and yet we're unsure of how to breathe. Perhaps the animals are better off than us!"

Finally, I asked them to place a hand on their stomach and relax. "Now, what happens when you inhale?"

The room filled with smiles as most participants realized that the stomach expands—goes out—when we breathe in. However, one young man, still unconvinced, loudly declared, "In!"

The session ended with camaraderie and a newfound awareness of both breath and the need for balance. Relaxation wasn't a "swear word" anymore—it was the key to sustaining their service.

#5 Why Don't We Relax?

The aversion to relaxation stems from deep-rooted conditioning that equates hard work with success and happiness. From a young age, we are taught to believe that relentless effort is the key to achieving our goals, leaving little room for rest. Our desperation for happiness drives us to overwork, and we convince ourselves that relaxation is a luxury we can't afford. The overwork of the body inevitably spills over into the mind—we begin to equate overthinking with productivity!

At its core, this refusal to relax is tied to a mistaken sense of self-worth. Many of us derive our value from external achievements—earning more money, owning a bigger house, or driving a fancy car. To attain these symbols of success, we feel compelled to struggle and toil.

Another barrier to relaxation is our insatiable desire for "more." Materialism fuels this constant chase, and comparison with others only worsens the cycle. Envy whispers, *"If they have it, I must have it too."* Ironically, while we yearn for love and connection, our actions prioritize accomplishments over relationships. Insecurity compounds the issue, with fears like *"I won't have enough for old age"* driving us to perpetually seek more.

The solution lies in shifting our paradigm: instead of defining our worth by what we do, we should root it in who we belong to. We belong to God—Krishna—and our worth comes from His unconditional love. Krishna does not judge us by the goals we achieve but by our sincere desire to love and serve Him and His devotees.

When we connect to God and experience His love in our hearts, an immense sense of contentment fills our lives. Recognizing that we are dear to Krishna allows us to step off the treadmill of worldly achievement. Instead of letting work define us, we can find value in our relationship with Him. And to nurture that connection, we need to make time for relaxation, prayer, meditation, and inviting His grace into our hearts—even as we fulfill our duties in the material world.

Interestingly, even spiritual practitioners can fall into the same trap as materialists. They may view themselves as sinful or fallen and believe they must work tirelessly to make spiritual progress. This mistaken pursuit of worth through excessive spiritual practices or services can lead to the same delusion, albeit under the guise of devotion.

While humility and a sense of inadequacy are essential in spiritual life, they should never overshadow the truth that God loves us unconditionally. That love is our ultimate worth. A sincere prayer, such as *"Please accept me, Lord, and allow me to feel Your love in my heart,"* can help us trust in God and relax internally.

This principle is beautifully illustrated in the story of Lord Rama's monkey army. As the *vanaras* (monkeys) toiled to build a bridge to Lanka, by carrying huge rocks, a tiny squirrel worked alongside them, carrying pebbles. A *vanara* mocked her seemingly insignificant effort, questioning her contribution compared to the gigantic mountain stones the monkeys were moving.

The squirrel replied humbly, *"I am serving Lord Rama to the best of my ability, just as you are."* Amused, the monkey dismissed her work as trivial and unworthy.

Seeing this exchange, Lord Rama stepped in. Picking up the squirrel, he turned to the monkey and said, *"I see no difference between her effort and yours. She is offering me her best, and I accept her loving service with gratitude. To you, her work may seem small, but I see it as a precious, sacred gift, given with complete devotion. I am purchased by her love."*

In our spiritual journey, some of us may be like Hanuman, capable of monumental tasks. Others may be like the squirrel, offering smaller contributions. What matters is not the size of our effort but the sincerity and love with which we offer it.

When we find our worth in our relationship with Krishna, we no longer feel pressured to measure up to worldly or even spiritual standards of achievement. Instead, we can relax, feeling content and secure in His love. This inner peace allows us to serve with joy and purpose, knowing that Krishna accepts whatever we offer with a heart full of devotion.

#6 Relax About Relaxing! From Struggle to Surrender

Some people become desperate to relax. "Yes, I need to relax. Can you suggest three or four ways to do it?" If you are working hard to relax, the first step is to release that effort. You need to relax about relaxing!

We live in a world that's constantly on the go, always filled with challenges and competition. We're always battling something, whether it is work, finances, or relationships. When we finally realize we need to slow down and relax, another struggle arises in our minds—"How do I relax perfectly?" "Is there a relaxation method that will recharge me in five minutes?" "I can spare ten minutes to relax; is there an effective tool for that?"

These questions reflect a deeper issue—our innate desire for control. We typically focus on controlling our external lives: our jobs, finances, and relationships. Now, we want to control our inner worlds as well. But in both cases, we are still trapped in struggle. True relaxation is the opposite of control; it is a precursor to surrender. It is the ability to release our struggle and align ourselves to a force beyond ourselves.

Scientists estimate that this planet is at least 13.8 billion years old. While we could debate the technical reality of this, one thing is for sure—life has been extant on this planet for a very long time. People lived, fought, had sex, and ate a variety of food even before 1973 (my year of birth), and much after 2073, they would continue to sing, dance, murder, and defecate. The planet would be abuzz with billions of living entities. Their tragedies and glory would fill newsroom debates and history would be rewritten. And I better realize soon enough that I am nobody in this creation and can't alter the course of history. Even if I decide otherwise, Venus and Mars would rotate around the sun; seasons would change despite my strong protests. I am nobody, yet I resist and struggle and desire to change the settings of this universe.

When it rains heavily, you might lament, "I wish it wouldn't rain so I could go outside." But the reality of the rain is beyond your control. So, why not simply declare, "I accept this rain!" This act of acceptance is, in essence, surrender—and relaxation.

"I am tired. I accept that my body and mind are in pain." The moment you accept your reality—your fallibility—you will begin to feel relaxed. This is because you are no longer resisting your true place in the universe. You accept your smallness, not as a burden, but as a beautiful truth. In that moment, you surrender to the flow of life and depend on a higher power (Krishna) to guide you, accepting His will.

Thus, the first step in relaxation is not to 'try' or 'struggle' to relax, but to *allow* yourself to relax. If you are 'struggling' to relax, you have missed the point. The key is to be *willing* to relax.

#7 From 'Trying' to 'Allowing'

My daily schedule is often packed, and even my spiritual practices are tightly bound by time. Ironically, activities like chanting and meditation—meant to uplift the spirit—sometimes feel like items to check off a to-do list. In these moments of overwhelm, I occasionally abandon all obligations, spiritual or otherwise, and sit alone in our temple hall. The sacred energy of prayer and belonging within the temple creates a unique space for reconnecting with God. In the quiet, I relax and simply *be*.

When I notice my mind wandering, I gently remind myself, *"It's okay for the mind to wander."* With that acceptance, I return to Krishna with love, whispering in my heart, *"I love you, Krishna."* This simple, loving acknowledgment reorients my mind. I breathe deeply, relax, and allow the presence of the Lord to naturally fill my consciousness.

Moments later, I might catch myself planning my evening class or drafting a response to an email. When I realize this, I remind myself again, *"It's okay. My mind is preparing for a class, and that's fine. Now, I return to you, Krishna. I seek your love."* With this awareness and gentle acceptance, my mind quietens, opening itself to Krishna's grace.

Often, we become so addicted to *doing* that we struggle to simply *be*, or to allow the Lord to enter our hearts. For example, during a morning class, when a speaker shares something profound, my first instinct is to write it down or memorize it for later use in my lectures. One day, I decided to let go of that habit. Instead of trying to capture every word, I simply basked in the speaker's presence and the sincerity of the audience. I let each word wash over me without forcing attentiveness.

Yes, my mind wandered, but that was okay. When I noticed it, I gently brought myself back to the class, first acknowledging my smallness and imperfection. There was nothing wrong with me. I didn't have to achieve anything. I had already reached my destination: I was home, sitting in the sacred presence of the *Śrīmad-Bhāgavatam.*

Occasionally, when a philosophical point struck me deeply, I would pause, breathe, and offer a sincere prayer to Krishna, thanking Him for allowing me to receive this wisdom. In those moments, I might lose track of the speaker's ongoing words, but that was okay too. When I returned to the class, it was with a sense of gratitude, having let the previous point settle in my heart.

By the end of the hour-long class, I didn't remember everything, but what I truly absorbed stayed with me, nourishing my soul. Previously, the wisdom would have been quickly jotted down, later recycled in my teachings—a mere mental exercise. But now, by slowing down and hearing with my heart, I allowed the sound vibrations to penetrate deeply. I was no longer *trying* to practice spiritual life. I was *allowing* Krishna consciousness to flow into my heart.

This reminds me of a story about a hunter who traps a monkey using a jar filled with chickpeas (*channa*) and nuts. The jar's opening is narrow, and when the monkey grabs the food, his clenched hand gets stuck. He cannot free himself, no matter how hard he tries, because he refuses to let go of the bait.

Aren't we, too, like the monkey, tightly holding on to our

desires and attachments? I'm not suggesting we abandon them entirely. But could we, even briefly each day, release our grip on the "*channa*" and free our minds from their bindings?

Breathing is the key. Conscious, intentional breaths allow us to loosen our hold on the mental clutter—the "nuts" in our minds—and free ourselves from the jar of material consciousness. Through mindful breathing, we open the door to our spiritual journey.

#8 If I Relax, Would I Lose Focus?

As a teenager, I fancied myself a leg spinner and dreamed of playing cricket for India. But my cricketing aspirations never went beyond casual games with school friends. Years later, after life had tempered my youthful ambitions, I stumbled upon an interview with Shane Warne, the legendary Australian leg spinner. Known for his ability to spin the ball viciously and leave even the best batsmen in awe, Warne revealed the secret behind his mastery: relaxation.

Warne shared that he held the ball lightly and stayed relaxed as he approached the crease. Gripping the ball too tightly or stiffening his body, he explained, would leave him vulnerable to the batsman. By maintaining a loose grip, he could stride up calmly and stay in control of the mental game. Warne emphasized that a relaxed bowler is better equipped to execute their plans at the critical moment.

Reading that interview, I wished I had known this wisdom in my younger days. Back then, I approached every delivery with intense focus but without easing my stride or grip. My overexertion became my downfall. I thought my intensity was helping me concentrate, but in reality, my tension was sabotaging my performance. It was only much later in life that I realized the importance of breathing and relaxing to achieve better results.

Though I learned this sacred lesson from cricket belatedly, I began applying it in other areas of life. For example, before and after I give classes or attend management meetings, I pause, pray, and consciously relax my body. This simple practice helps me stay in control of my emotions, think clearly, and contribute meaningfully.

Even in high-stakes environments, relaxation is a powerful tool. The United States Navy SEALS, among the world's most elite special forces, are trained to perform under extreme pressure. Their missions often involve capturing or eliminating high-value targets with astonishing precision. Despite their rigorous training and the intense nature of their work, SEALS practice relaxation techniques like *sama vritti pranayama*—also known as "box breathing." This method involves inhaling for four counts, holding the breath for four counts, exhaling for four counts, and holding again for four counts. By regulating their breathing, SEALS improve their physiological responses and remain calm even in life-threatening situations.

This principle applies to everyone, whether you're an office worker, homemaker, or student. Practicing deep, conscious breathing helps slow down your heart rate, deepen concentration, and stay grounded. Paradoxically, by relaxing more, you concentrate better.

On the other hand, staying busy all day doesn't necessarily mean you're focused or effective. True productivity often emerges when the brain operates at lower frequencies, such as alpha waves, which promote calmness, creativity, and clarity.

Relaxation isn't a loss of focus—it is the foundation for achieving it.

#9 Is Breathing a Spiritual Activity?

No, breathing isn't inherently a spiritual activity, nor is it a core meditation practice in Bhakti-Yoga. However, it is one of the most fundamental building blocks for effective living. Whether one is a spiritualist or not, learning to relax is essential for achieving anything meaningful. In fact, relaxation serves as a precursor to meditation.

Once, after teaching a group of young people some basic breathing techniques, a senior member of the community posed a provocative question: *"If this isn't directly spiritual, why are you teaching it? Do you have the mandate to speak on non-Bhakti-Yoga practices? And isn't this compromised approach to spirituality a step back in your own journey?"*

I paused to reflect before responding.

"As a young monk, I chanted *Hare Krishna* on my *japa* beads, primarily seeking peace. Back then, my *japa* was the means, and peace was the end I sought. But that wasn't a very noble purpose for spiritual practice. Today, I seek peace as a *means* to chant better, to connect with Krishna more deeply and lovingly. Now, the Holy Names of Krishna are my ultimate goal. If breathing and relaxation help me chant with greater focus and devotion, they have a place in my practice."

His eyes widened in understanding, and he asked, "But if these techniques are so helpful, why haven't Srila Prabhupada or other great Bhakti saints emphasized breathing or relaxation?"

"It was a done deal back then," I replied. "People lived simpler, more harmonious lives, naturally aligned with the rhythms of nature. They didn't need reminders to slow down or reconnect with themselves. Today, however, our fast-paced, disconnected lifestyles necessitate such reminders. Before we can connect with God, we need to reconnect with ourselves."

I reflected on my childhood in a small South Indian village. Every evening, my grandparents would take me to the fields, where we'd sit quietly under the vast open sky. As the sun set, they often had little to say. The silence they shared with each other, with me in the center occasionally glancing at them, was an expression of love and togetherness. Sometimes they would greet a passing villager or briefly discuss an errand, but mostly, they just sat and looked out at the expanse. When it was time to return home, they rose quietly and walked me back, still without many words.

That daily dose of silent relaxation was their tonic—a way to process life's inevitable challenges with grace. Life wasn't easier then than it is now. They had their share of struggles, but without smartphones or constant distractions, they faced their worries head-on. They embraced their pain, dealt kindly with themselves and others, and moved forward with dignity.

Today, we pride ourselves on technological advancements and instant access to entertainment and information. Yet this constant stimulation often leaves us restless, disconnected, and empty. We seem to be running away from ourselves, perpetually grappling with an inner void. Perhaps we don't always need answers to our suffering. Sometimes, we just need to sit with it, make peace with it, and breathe.

This quiet space of peace becomes the foundation for our spiritual journey. As Krishna tells Arjuna in the *Bhagavad Gita* (2.66):

> *"One who is not connected with the Supreme [in Krishna consciousness] can have neither transcendental intelligence nor a steady mind, without which there is no possibility of peace. And how can there be any happiness without peace?"*

Breathing and relaxation may not be explicitly spiritual, but they create the conditions for peace—and peace is the fertile ground in which spirituality flourishes.

#10 Breathing and Relaxation in the Bhakti-Yoga Tradition

Srila Sanatana Goswami, a prominent saint in the Bhakti-Yoga tradition, once served as the prime minister of Bengal under Nawab Hussain Shah in the early sixteenth century. Despite his position of incredible wealth and power, he renounced everything to dedicate his life to serving God. As a mendicant devotee, he lived in the sacred town of Vrindavan, where he wrote devotional scriptures, built temples, served local villagers, and absorbed himself in the practices of Bhakti-Yoga. A key disciple of Lord Chaitanya, Srila Sanatana Goswami authored many works, including *Sri Hari-Bhakti-Vilas*, a guidebook on the etiquette and lifestyle of devotees.

In the fifth chapter, or *Vilasa*, of *Sri Hari-Bhakti-Vilas*, Srila Sanatana Goswami discusses the science of meditating on the

Lord and includes descriptions of breathing exercises. Though often overlooked in contemporary discussions of Bhakti-Yoga, these breathing practices underscore the importance of cultivating a calm and focused mind as a foundation for devotional service.

Similarly, Srila Prabhupada, the founder of ISKCON, exemplified balance in his spiritual practice. Though widely known as a tireless preacher who, even in his eighties, travelled the globe, opened temples, and managed countless responsibilities, his life was also marked by an equilibrium rooted in *sattva*—the mode of goodness.

Despite his rigorous schedule, Srila Prabhupada took deliberate steps to stay grounded. He received a daily oil massage in the afternoons, took morning walks with his disciples, enjoyed candid conversations, and ate lunch quietly, alone. In the early 1960s, while living in Vrindavan and translating the *Śrīmad-Bhāgavatam*, he maintained a rhythm of visiting prominent Krishna temples every morning and evening. Even during the last decade of his life, when he travelled extensively, he wrote through the early hours of the morning, and handled management challenges. He made time each day to connect deeply with himself, Krishna, and others.

This balance—between service to the world and connection with self and God—was a hallmark of his ability to perform seemingly relentless tasks with grace.

One day in Vrindavan, Srila Prabhupada spent several hours conversing and laughing with an elderly man. Since most of his disciples present were Westerners, they couldn't follow the Hindi conversation. After the man left, curiosity bubbled over.

"Was he your doctor, Srila Prabhupada?" one disciple asked.

"No," replied Srila Prabhupada.

"Was he your Godbrother?"

Again, Srila Prabhupada said no.

"Maybe he was a local temple priest?"

"No."

Perplexed, the disciple finally asked, "Who was he, Srila Prabhupada?"

Srila Prabhupada smiled warmly and replied, "He is my friend."

This sweet exchange reflects the essence of Bhakti-Yoga: a life of balance, connection, and meaningful relationships. Srila Prabhupada's ability to remain grounded, even while undertaking monumental spiritual tasks, serves as a timeless lesson.

#11 My Challenges in Spiritual Life and How Relaxation Helped

"One who is regulated in eating, recreation, sleeping, and working can mitigate all sorrows by practicing yoga."

—*The Bhagavad Gita* (6.17)

"Our entire process is recreation," Srila Prabhupada once emphatically declared in response to a reporter who had asked how devotees relax and balance their lives. For years, I struggled to understand the deeper meaning of this statement.

Why did I feel stressed while performing devotional service? Why did the very activities meant to uplift my soul sometimes leave me drained?

Despite my enthusiasm, I found myself mentally exhausted after days of uninterrupted temple programs and services. When weeks passed without a break, I pushed on, mistakenly believing that because Bhakti-Yoga is transcendental, I shouldn't feel tired. However, my body and mind told a different story.

I began to hit a wall. My brain felt numb, my strength waned, and even the most basic tasks became monumental. Some mornings, I couldn't summon the will to get out of bed. I felt irritable and found it difficult to manage simple routines like taking medicine or bathing.

The breaking point came when my resolve to chant attentive *japa*—the daily meditation on Krishna's Holy Names—crumbled. As a formally initiated ISKCON devotee, I had vowed to chant 16 rounds of the *Hare Krishna* mantra on my beads each day. This sacred practice takes about two hours, and it is the foundation of our spiritual life. Yet despite my commitment, I found myself unable to pay attention to my chanting.

As a full-time teacher of Krishna consciousness, this inner struggle felt like a betrayal of everything I stood for. How could I teach others the joy of Bhakti-Yoga while drowning in misery myself?

I feared I was in *maya*—illusion—or even on the verge of a psychological breakdown. Desperately, I resolved to double down on hearing and chanting, believing that greater effort would lead to a breakthrough. After all, hadn't Srila Prabhupada said that Bhakti is recreation and devotees don't take holidays?

But my mind and senses rebelled. The harder I pushed, the more resistance I encountered.

When even hearing and chanting became unbearable, I sought advice from friends and mentors. Some suggested that I was committing offenses, which explained my lack of taste for Krishna's Holy Names. Others encouraged me to fight harder, pay closer attention to my practices, and struggle through the discomfort.

But I was already struggling—and I was losing.

I had heard many times that Krishna helps sincere devotees at the time of death. But I didn't want help *then*—I needed help *now*.

A tired brain and the guilt trap

The harder I fought my mind to stay focused on my spiritual activities, the more exhausted I felt. And with that exhaustion came regret and guilt. A relentless voice whispered: "You're not sincere. You're bad."

But then I noticed something curious—this condemnation only arose when my mind struggled, not when my body did. For example, after walking the 21-kilometer *parikrama* (circumambulation) of the sacred Govardhan Hill, my legs would ache terribly, and I'd be unable to take another step. Yet I never blamed myself for the physical exhaustion. I didn't conclude that I was insincere or inadequate because I couldn't keep walking.

However, when my brain got tired—after days of intense work or mental strain—it felt as though my mind had walked a marathon. If I then struggled to chant attentively or engage in devotional practices, the guilt would hit me like a storm: "You're a sinner. You're failing. You're not serious about your spiritual life." To redeem myself, I would force even more chanting or other spiritual activities, as if punishing myself for my perceived inadequacy.

The truth I missed was so simple: the brain, like the body, is a physical organ. Just as legs ache after overexertion, the brain, too, can tire when overworked.

But instead of resting, I plunged into self-criticism, making my plight worse. I was gaslighting myself, compounding emotional pain with harsh judgment. I failed to see that my inability to chant attentively or my lack of enthusiasm for devotional activities was not a sign of moral deficiency or insincerity—it was just fatigue.

Sadly, many sincere practitioners fall into this same trap. They start their Krishna consciousness journey with sweet enthusiasm, only to end up hating themselves for "lacking taste" in spiritual practices. When we constantly tell ourselves, "I'm bad," we inadvertently reinforce a destructive cycle.

The mind doesn't understand the nuance of rejection or unwillingness. When you tell yourself, "I'm bad," the mind only processes the affirmation. It begins to seek out the very activities associated with being "bad." It doesn't recognize that you are trying to reject those behaviors; it simply obeys the narrative.

This is why negative self-talk is so dangerous. It feeds a cycle of guilt, shame, and behavior that drags us further away from the values we cherish. If I keep reinforcing "I'm sinful" in my mind, I will be drawn to actions that confirm this belief.

To break free, we must replace "I'm bad" with compassion and understanding. Recognize fatigue for what it is—an invitation to rest, not a judgment of character. By doing so, we give ourselves the grace to recover and return to our spiritual practices with renewed energy and sincerity.

Our brain, much like our legs, is a physical organ that tires with overuse. Just as running on aching legs leads to injury, forcing the brain to pay more attention when it is exhausted can lead to mental fatigue or burnout.

In spiritual practice, we often hear that *paying attention* or being present is key to success, especially in chanting the *Hare Krishna* mantra. But how can we stay attentive, reap the benefits of chanting, and still avoid exhaustion and mental fatigue?

For that we need to understand the two types of *attention.*

#12 Two Types of Attention: Voluntary and Involuntary

1. Voluntary attention (struggle)

This type of attention requires effort. For example, if you're chanting but distractions arise—such as people talking or phone notifications—you must consciously pull your mind back to the task. Voluntary attention involves choosing one focus and saying "no" to all other distractions. This kind of attention can feel like you're swimming upstream, especially during *japa* meditation for many *Hare Krishna* devotees. The constant effort to redirect the mind is tiring and can lead to brain fatigue.

2. Involuntary attention (ease)

In contrast, involuntary attention flows naturally and effortlessly. It arises when you're fully absorbed in an activity that resonates with you. For instance, when I write my morning journal, I find it easy to remain focused. I don't need to battle distractions or force myself to concentrate. Similarly, a friend of mine, Anand Vrindavan, could chant *Hare Krishna* all day and feel rejuvenated, while I felt drained after two hours. For him, chanting was an activity of involuntary attention, while for me, it required voluntary effort.

This realization led me to create a list of Krishna-conscious activities that demanded *involuntary attention* from me. Along with journaling, I found breathing exercises, deity worship, and *kirtans* (devotional singing) to be my sources of easy attention.

Should we embrace the struggle?

A close friend once suggested that I should deliberately engage more in activities that required voluntary attention. "You need to enjoy the struggle of Bhakti-Yoga!" he declared. While I respected his perspective, I disagreed. Struggle involves continually redirecting a wandering mind, which naturally tires the brain. Mental fatigue, unlike physical exhaustion, is often ignored and can lead to irritability, burnout, or even actions that betray one's values.

Navigating guilt and shame

When we fail to meet our spiritual standards, guilt often arises. This is not necessarily bad; guilt can motivate us to return to our values. However, it becomes problematic when it transforms into shame.

- **Guilt**: "I did a bad thing."
- **Shame**: "I am a bad person."

While guilt focuses on a specific action and encourages correction, shame attacks your identity, making you believe that failure defines who you are. This emotional shift is harmful, especially in a fast-paced life where unresolved shame amplifies mental fatigue and perpetuates a cycle of self-condemnation.

The other extreme: Lethargy masquerading as honesty

Some people swing to the opposite extreme. They accept their shortcomings as permanent and stop striving to improve. Mistaking lethargy or apathy for honesty, they declare, "This is who I am," and refuse to aim higher. True honesty, however, means acknowledging where you are while making a sincere effort to move forward. It is about progress, not complacency.

To thrive in spiritual practice, recognize the difference between voluntary and involuntary attention. Engage more in activities that naturally absorb your focus to rejuvenate your mind.

Simple ways to relax and enjoy spiritual life

The solution to burnout in spiritual practice lies in discovering your unique ways to spend time in activities that require *involuntary attention.* These activities should align with healthy, life-enhancing principles and help you rejuvenate.

For me, *japa* meditation is a daily duty that often requires voluntary, or "struggle" attention. On the other hand, journaling and nature walks are effortless for me; they rejuvenate my mind and spirit. Over time, I have embraced semi-spiritual activities as tools to connect with Krishna. As

Rupa Goswami, a principal teacher of Bhakti-Yoga, advised in the sixteenth century:

> *"Yena kena prakarena manah Krishna nivesayet."*
> (Somehow or other, fix your mind on Krishna.)

And if breathing and journal writing helps to fix the mind on God, accept the practice happily.

The power of semi-spiritual activities

Semi-spiritual activities such as poetry, journaling, philosophy, and nature walks engage my easy attention, helping me relax and stay mindful. Surprisingly, these moments of effortless mindfulness have positively impacted my direct spiritual practices. For example:

- *My japa meditation has improved in quality*
- *My focus during scripture study lasts longer*
- *I feel more present and connected in social settings*

Even during simple moments—like observing raindrops on a window, marveling at a centipede, or watching grasshoppers in my hometown—I found myself deeply engaged. I stopped forcing myself to derive spiritual meaning from everything I saw. Instead, I embraced the act of being present as part of Krishna consciousness.

The importance of relaxation

Designating daily time for relaxation—during bathing, eating, or casual conversations—has well-documented benefits. While ancient philosophers extolled the virtues of spending time in nature, science has only recently confirmed its effects. Since the 1990s, research has shown that observing natural phenomena like clouds, rustling leaves, or waterfalls rejuvenates the mind. Yoga has a similar impact.

When I began incorporating relaxation practices such as oil massages, poetry, and journaling into my routine, I found Bhakti-Yoga more relishable. Although Bhakti is a transcendental process and not dependent on anything material, a relaxed brain makes devotional activities more enjoyable. For most sincere practitioners, devotional service requires voluntary attention—making conscious choices, focusing, and exerting effort. Without intentional relaxation in a space of no struggle, we risk burnout.

Expanding the circle of easy attention

Many people have a very small "circle of easy attention," meaning they rarely relax. Conversely, their "circle of struggle attention" is much larger, leaving them stressed and fatigued. The key to balance is simple:

- Identify activities that naturally engage your mind with minimal effort
- Expand your circle of involuntary attention by incorporating these activities into your routine
- Recognize that relaxation is not a luxury but an essential foundation for sustained spiritual growth

By making space for effortless attention, we create a fertile ground for our spiritual practices to flourish, making Bhakti-Yoga a more joyous and enriching experience.

#13 Does Watching Movies or YouTube Reels Really Relax Us?

Is binge-watching on Netflix or scrolling through YouTube reels truly relaxing? At first glance, it may seem so—watching a movie or short clips demands no effort, no struggle to focus, and even allows us to lose track of time. But does this kind of absorption genuinely aid our spiritual pursuits?

The nature of true relaxation

Spiritual life seeks to connect us to a metaphysical reality—a realm that transcends the temporary nature of this world. The physical reality we perceive through our senses has a beginning and an end, like the apartment you live in, the clothes you wear, or even your body. The metaphysical reality, however, is eternal and unchanging.

This is why we feel a sense of peace in nature—by the ocean, under the moon, or surrounded by mountains. These elements, in their apparent timelessness, resonate with the undying nature of the self. Bhakti-Yoga practices, such as chanting the Holy Names or studying scriptures like the *Śrīmad-Bhāgavatam*, gently elevate a practitioner from the physical to the metaphysical plane.

But when we spend hours glued to electronic screens, we are drawn not to the metaphysical or even the physical, but to a virtual reality. This world of flickering lights and endless content offers, at best, fleeting dopamine hits. The joy of hiking in a forest or the satisfaction of a good workout involves active engagement and effort, while watching a movie or scrolling reels is a passive form of relaxation that disconnects us from both the physical and metaphysical realities.

Active vs. Passive relaxation

Passive relaxation, like binge-watching, silences the mind momentarily but doesn't truly relax it. It is akin to taking a painkiller during a heart attack—it dulls the symptom without addressing the root cause. True relaxation requires facing reality, sitting with discomfort, and allowing the mind to wander before gently bringing it back to the present moment.

When we choose active relaxation—reading, meditating, walking in nature, or reflecting—we align ourselves with the physical reality, which serves as a launchpad for transcending to the metaphysical plane. For example, reading a book, especially one with spiritual content, engages the imagination and deepens our connection to the subject.

Consider the difference between reading a *Harry Potter* novel and watching a movie adaptation. While a movie provides instant gratification with visuals and sound, reading the book allows you to create your own imagery. Your brain actively constructs the scenes, fostering creativity and deeper engagement.

Similarly, reading spiritual texts like *Krishna: The Supreme Personality of Godhead* can transport the mind to divine pastimes. Instead of being a passive viewer, you become the director of the narrative in your mind. For instance, as Krishna and Balarama enter Mathura, the streets, the people, and the vibrant welcome they receive come alive in your imagination. This active engagement helps your mind connect to Krishna's transcendental personality, infusing it with spiritual energy.

Finding a balance

It is natural to seek relief when faced with intense challenges or suffering. Smartphones and movies can seem like a quick fix, but they don't address deeper issues. They provide momentary escape but leave the mind unfulfilled and often more fatigued.

Spiritual practices, like "medicine," offer a lasting solution. They heal at the root level, gradually transforming the mind and heart.

If you're tempted to turn to movies or reels for relief, consider setting aside time for active relaxation that truly nourishes your soul. Walk in nature, listen to soothing *kirtans*, or engage in mindful journaling. While these activities may not offer the instant thrill of a dopamine spike, they leave the mind more refreshed and connected to higher realities.

True relaxation is not about escaping the present but embracing it. In doing so, we not only rejuvenate but also prepare ourselves to better engage in spiritual practices, moving closer to the eternal metaphysical reality that is the ultimate source of peace.

#14 The *'Doing'* vs. *'Being'* Modes - How Can We Make Spiritual Practices Relaxing?

In the *Bhagavad Gita* (9.2), Krishna explains that spiritual practices are joyful, provide direct experience of truth, and offer eternal benefits. Yet many practitioners often struggle with them, losing the joy of simply *'being'* with the Lord. This disconnect—the proverbial slip between the cup and the lip—can be traced back to our over-reliance on the *'doing'* mode.

The *'doing'* mode: Necessary but draining

The *'doing'* mode governs our analytical, problem-solving, and action-oriented behaviors. It is indispensable for navigating the complexities of life, whether it is planning a grocery list, responding to emails, or managing relationships. However, constantly operating in this mode can be mentally exhausting.

When the brain is in a perpetual *'doing'* mode, it uses up its limited mental reserves. This often leads to insomnia, stress, and burnout as we carry unresolved struggles into our downtime. The irony is that even in spiritual practices, we can unknowingly carry this mode, turning what should be a relaxing communion with the divine into yet another task to perfect.

The *'being'* mode: A gateway to relaxation

The *'being'* mode, in contrast, is characterized by mindfulness, presence, and surrender. It is about accepting the moment without resistance or judgment. Instead of striving to control a situation, the *'being'* mode invites us to connect with it.

When in this state, we replace control with acceptance, and struggle with surrender. For instance, a conversation becomes an opportunity to listen without formulating responses, and meditation transforms into a chance to simply be present, rather than perfect.

Shifting between the modes

The *'doing'* and *'being'* modes are not determined by what we do outwardly but by our internal consciousness. A person lying in bed can still be stuck in the *'doing'* mode, overthinking and planning, while a busy CEO can remain in the *'being'* mode by letting go of outcomes and staying present.

The key is knowing when to switch. If you leave the tap running after a shower, you waste water; if you leave the lights on all day, you waste electricity. Similarly, staying in *'doing'* mode when it is unnecessary drains mental energy. The ability to "turn off" and enter the *'being'* mode is what helps us conserve energy and find balance.

Breaking free from the *'doing'* addiction

Many of us are stuck in the *'doing'* mode out of habit. Society often glorifies constant thinking and productivity, equating rest with laziness. This mindset makes it challenging to embrace the *'being'* mode, even in spiritual practices.

However, to experience the grace and joy of spiritual life, we must learn to let go of the need for control and perfection. Instead of struggling to "achieve" meditation, for example, we can approach it with curiosity and non-judgment, simply returning to the present moment whenever the mind wanders.

A personal example: Parenting with the *'being'* mode

Manish Agarwal, a friend, shared a transformational experience:

"When I became a father, I was overwhelmed by fear—fear of my baby choking, falling, or being harmed. My wife, too, was

struggling emotionally, and I felt like a failure as both a husband and a father.

"One day, I attended a seminar by an ISKCON devotee on the 'doing' and 'being' modes. I realized I was trapped in the 'doing' mode, constantly trying to control everything. Inspired, I decided to experiment with the 'being' mode.

"I began observing my baby with curiosity instead of fear. Her tiny fingers, her attempts to make sense of the world—it all became mesmerizing. Parenting transformed from a chore into an adventure. Seeing our daughter crawl one day, and her baby steps and the first words she uttered, are all permanently etched in my memory. Also, my wife noticed I didn't panic during her mood swings—I was accepting and allowing the situation to be what it is, without trying to drastically alter it. Eventually, she, too, learnt the 'being' mode methods and today, as we celebrate our daughter's fifth birthday, we are enjoying the struggles of parenthood."

Practical tips to embrace the *'being'* mode

1. **Let go of perfection:** In meditation or chanting, release the desire to perform perfectly. Simply return to the practice with acceptance when the mind wanders.
2. **Focus on the present:** Bring your attention to the here and now. Observe sensations, sounds, or sights without judgment or analysis.
3. **Adopt curiosity:** Approach life with an open, childlike curiosity. Instead of controlling, allow yourself to be influenced by the moment.
4. **Relax into surrender:** Trust in a higher power. Let go of struggles that are beyond your control and be open to receiving solutions rather than forcing them.

#15 Radhanath Swami's Lessons on the *'Being'* Mode

On several occasions, Radhanath Swami Maharaj has imparted profound lessons on the need to transcend time, at least for a part of the day, and be in the *'being'* state. Two particular incidents remain etched in my memory as vivid examples of this practice:

1. Eating sweet rice slowly and prayerfully

In June 1998, around 800 devotees from Mumbai accompanied Radhanath Swami Maharaj on our annual pilgrimage to the holy town of Jagannath Puri. One day, we traveled to Remuna, a town approximately 450 kilometers north of Puri. Remuna is known for the Khirchor Gopinath Temple, where the Supreme Lord, in His form as Gopinath, stole sweet rice (kheer) for His devotee, Madhavendra Puri. Since that pastime in the fifteenth century, devotees have been coming to Remuna and purchasing a cup of this divine sweet rice prasad.

On our visit, Radhanath Swami Maharaj narrated this beautiful pastime in the temple courtyard. His narration was slow and deliberate, paying attention to the smallest details of how Madhavendra Puri received the cup of sweet rice from the Lord through the priest. It was as if we were transported five hundred years into the past. As Maharaj spoke, we were all captivated by the story, fully absorbed in the moment.

However, the *yatra* organizers were anxious about the time. They had reassured the bus drivers that we would leave Remuna by 3 p.m., ensuring they could finish their day by

10 p.m. But Maharaj, lost in the flow of his class, was oblivious to the ticking clock. The organizers tried to urge him to wrap up, sending notes and reminders about the bus schedules. But Maharaj continued, unperturbed.

As the class went on, the *yatra* coordinator, Sanat Kumar Prabhu, tried everything he could to pacify the bus drivers, who were growing impatient. Meanwhile, Maharaj remained absorbed in his teaching, and the devotees continued to listen, enjoying every moment. After a few more attempts, Sanat Kumar had an idea to speed things up: he arranged for the eight hundred small pots of sweet rice to be distributed evenly across all the buses, so everyone could honor the prasad during the return journey.

Finally, around 7 p.m., Maharaj concluded his class. But just as the organizers breathed a sigh of relief, Maharaj announced that we would now honor the sweet rice. The devotees cheered, and Sanat Kumar proudly announced that he had arranged for everyone to receive their prasad in the buses. However, Maharaj, with a quiet yet firm tone, instructed that all the sweet rice pots be brought out, and instead of eating immediately, we were to meditate on Madhavendra Puri, for whom the Lord had stolen the kheer.

Maharaj guided us through a slow and conscious meditation, asking us to taste the sweet rice, one finger at a time, while meditating on Lord Krishna. The entire process lasted nearly an hour. While the devotees were deeply immersed in this transcendent experience, Sanat Kumar, ever-conscious of the time, couldn't help but feel the sweetness of the moment was lost on him. By the time we left Remuna at 9.30 p.m., we were more than six hours behind schedule.

At the end of the week-long *yatra*, during the feedback session, Sanat Kumar had planned to speak about the importance of adhering to timelines for smoother *yatra* management. He was shocked when, one after another, all thirty-five leaders and counselors shared how the Remuna experience had been the highlight of the pilgrimage. They spoke about the sweet rice meditation, saying it was the most therapeutic and enlightening spiritual experience they had ever had.

For Sanat Kumar, this was a revelation. What he had viewed as an inconvenience—the lack of punctuality—turned out to be the most meaningful experience for everyone else. By the time he spoke, he had been transformed. He realized that spiritual experiences are real, but to truly access the divine, one must transcend time and be present in the moment.

This experience taught him—and all of us—that we need to transcend the constraints of time and immerse ourselves fully in the present. Although we need to do the needful when it comes to punctuality and management of *yatras*, still it is only when we are present in our spiritual activity that we truly connect to the sacred.

2. Bangladesh *yatra* – "You are just not present!"

"Who's going to tell Guru Maharaj?" Gauranga whispered as a sense of discomfort crept over the dozen monks gathered for Radhanath Swami's class in the courtyard of the temple. It was the fifth hour of Maharaj's narration on the life and teachings of Narottam Das Thakur, a revered Vaishnava saint who spread the message of Bhakti-Yoga in Eastern India during the early sixteenth century.

Around twelve senior monks had accompanied Radhanath Swami on a pilgrimage through Eastern India, visiting the pastime places of many saints from our tradition. The Bangladesh leg of the journey had been particularly taxing. Long hours of road travel had exhausted the monks, and the food and water had caused some to suffer from indigestion. The late-night classes and *kirtans* had also left them with a significant sleep deficit. The discomfort was palpable.

Meanwhile, Radhanath Swami, who was nearly double the age of the other monks, remained full of energy, enthusiasm, and prayerfulness. He shared wisdom with fervor and led long *kirtans*, while the disciples struggled with exhaustion. They knew they had a long day ahead—traveling from Kheturi to Benapole, a journey of about 230 kilometers that would take no less than five hours. "If we don't end the class now and retire, tomorrow will be terrible. We need to rise by 3 a.m. and leave by 4," one monk said. But the question was: who would tell Maharaj to conclude the session? It was already 9 p.m., and they had begun the *satsanga* after lunch—nearly six hours ago.

Shyamananda, the most senior among them, gestured for everyone to relax. He indicated that he would speak to Maharaj if the class didn't end soon. But Maharaj seemed in a state of blissful trance, deeply absorbed in his narration. Finally, at 9.30 p.m., he stopped. The devotees felt a wave of relief—they could now prepare for the next day without having to interrupt their guru during his discourse. But their relief was short-lived. Maharaj pulled out his harmonium and announced that they would now sing and dance in *kirtan*. "Narottam Das Thakur's songs are spiritually potent," he said.

"If we sing them, especially here, where they were composed, we can access the spiritual world. So, let us chant for some time."

Instinctively, the devotees knew that "some time" meant no less than an hour. They looked toward Shyamananda, who, sensing the group's fatigue, volunteered to speak on their behalf. "Guru Maharaj," he whispered as he approached, "Tomorrow we have a long ride to Benapole, and the roads are difficult. We need to leave by 4 a.m. Is it possible to end today's session now and retire early?"

A long, uncomfortable silence fell over the courtyard as all eyes turned toward Radhanath Swami. After a moment, he smiled warmly and compassionately closed his harmonium. The students felt a mix of relief and guilt, as if they had failed to fully appreciate the sacred moment. Slowly, Maharaj rose and walked toward the group of monks. Looking at Shyamananda, he said softly yet firmly, "This is your problem—you are simply not present!"

The words hit them deeply. They realized that their minds had overwhelmed them with imaginary problems. By focusing on an insignificant issue—getting enough rest for the next day—they had missed out on the abundant spiritual energy present in the moment. They hadn't been fully present with Maharaj and the divine teachings he was imparting.

The next morning, as the group endured the bumpy ride to Benapole, Shyamananda quoted a passage from Srila Prabhupada's commentary on Narottam Das Thakur:

> *"The prayers of Narottam Das Thakur carry a sound above the material platform. They are directly from the spiritual*

realm. And there is no need to understand the language. It is like the sound of thunder—everyone can hear it, with no misunderstanding. Similarly, these songs are above the material platform, and they crack like thunder within your heart."

The quote sobered the group, and they made a silent promise to be more mindful during the rest of the *yatra*. They would absorb themselves more deeply in hearing and chanting the Lord's Holy Names with greater attention and prayer.

Prayer and chanting are powerful spiritual tools, central to the Bhakti tradition. They are a potent means to break the mind's constant tirade and propel us to a transcendental state.

We will explore this practice further in the next chapter.

Part C

Chanting

CHAPTER 3

Chanting

"Always chanting My glories, endeavoring with great determination, bowing down before Me, these great souls perpetually worship Me with devotion."

—*The Bhagavad Gita* (9.14)

At just 20 years old, Chris Matthews was a hardened criminal. Hooked on morphine since his early teens, he resorted to burglarizing drug stores to avoid the agony of withdrawal pains. Eventually caught, he was sentenced to eight years of rigorous imprisonment at Tennessee State Prison. Disgusted with himself and plagued by despair, Chris even contemplated ending his life. The weight of his choices bore down on him—he was now a father, and the thought of his daughter's judgment filled him with shame. Questions haunted him: *"How could I ever lead a normal life?", "Would I ever be free from my past?"* The more he thought and worried, the more he felt worthless.

In the isolation of his prison cell, Chris sought solace in spirituality. He experimented with various religious practices and meditation techniques, exploring Islam, Buddhism, Cabala, Advaita Vedanta, and Christianity. But peace remained elusive. Finally, in a moment of desperation, he poured out his heart in prayer: "Lord, I am lost. I remember You. Please help me."

A few days later, as if in answer, a *Hare Krishna* devotee from ISKCON's prison outreach program visited the facility. This devotee introduced Chris to the practice of chanting the *Hare Krishna* mantra using a string of 108 *japa* beads. Initially skeptical, Chris decided to try it. To his surprise, the simple act of chanting had a deep impact on his consciousness. A sense of peace began to enwrap his heart, and over time, his hardened demeanor softened.

Where once he had been numb to the brutality around him, Chris now found himself moved to tears by the transformative power of the Holy Names. Despite being confined within the four walls of a prison, he felt a sense of freedom—a freedom he had never experienced in his so-called "free" life, which he now recognized as a chain of bondage.

The more he chanted *Hare Krishna*, the more liberated he felt. Guided by ISKCON devotees, he learned the science of mantra meditation and the art of prayer. The practice reshaped his life, allowing him to rise above the quicksand of self-obsession and overthinking.

Eventually, Chris was released from prison, years before his sentence was completed. He joined ISKCON as a full-time teacher of meditation and now serves in ISKCON's prison ministry. His journey—from a prisoner to a prison minister—is a proof to the transformative power of chanting and prayer.

Chris is just one among countless individuals whose lives have been overwhelmingly changed by the practice of chanting God's Holy Names. When practiced with sincerity and patience, chanting and prayer have the power to permanently alter the course of our lives, lifting us beyond the confines of our worries and guiding us to a higher realm of consciousness.

Chris's remarkable transformation was palpable even to the prison authorities, who saw a man truly reformed. Today, Chris dedicates his life to helping others find the same freedom he once thought was impossible—a freedom born from the deepest devotion and the simplest prayer.

#1 What Happens to Overthinking When We Pray and Chant?

Every spiritual tradition embraces the practice of prayer and the chanting of God's Holy Names. The chanting of mantras not only helps calm the restless mind but also creates significant changes in the brain's neurological patterns. Many of us tread well-worn paths in our mental landscapes—loops of fear, anxiety, and destructive habits that only deepen our miseries. A culture of prayer challenges these patterns, offering us access to a power far greater than ourselves. When we pray, we entrust our worries to a benevolent God, accessible through the transcendental sound vibrations of His Holy Names.

When I first embarked on the path of Krishna consciousness, I made a habit of attending a spiritual gathering every Friday evening in Kandivali, a suburb in the north of Mumbai. On my return journey, traveling late at night on the local train, I would softly chant prayers on my beads. The *Hare Krishna* mantra, rooted in ancient Vedic scriptures, comprises sixteen words and is also known as the *Maha Mantra*:

Hare Krishna Hare Krishna Krishna Krishna Hare Hare
Hare Rama Hare Rama Rama Rama Hare Hare

From my study of the scriptures and attendance at spiritual classes, I learned that the *Hare Krishna* mantra is non-different from God Himself. When God manifests as sound, He appears as His Holy Names. Chanting sincerely, therefore, is equivalent to associating with the Supreme Lord. The more we chant, the more our heart is purified through this divine connection.

At first, I understood these teachings intellectually but hadn't yet experienced them deeply. Still, I continued chanting with faith and sincerity, trusting the process.

One day, I found myself particularly troubled by a recurring issue. No matter how hard I tried, I couldn't find a solution. My thoughts pulled me deeper into despair. Around this time, I had started chanting the *Hare Krishna* mantra every morning for an hour. Though my practice was often distracted, I persisted. While I felt moments of peace during my spiritual practices, my worries would resurface later in the day.

On one such Friday night, returning from an uplifting spiritual program, I sat alone in the train, softly chanting on my beads. As the train sped through the stations, I observed the endless crowds on the platforms. Passengers boarded and disembarked in a steady rhythm. At one station, a large, chaotic crowd surged into the train. Amid Mumbai's vibrant middle-class mosaic, I sat quietly, a detached observer. Suddenly, a realization struck me: *I am so insignificant, and my worries are equally insignificant. Just as these countless passengers mean nothing to anyone, my problems are but a drop in the ocean of existence.*

This insight lingered with me for days, reshaping my perspective. In a city of 15 million people, I felt tiny, and in the vastness of the cosmos, even more so. But curiously, this sense of insignificance didn't overwhelm me; instead, it was liberating. When I lifted my prayer beads and softly chanted the *Hare Krishna* mantra, a sense of peace flooded my heart. I felt sheltered.

On this night, as over five hundred people crammed into my coach, I noticed a mother struggling to balance herself while holding her sleeping baby. Despite the chaos, the child rested peacefully, oblivious to the pandemonium. Watching them, as I chanted, another wave of spiritual emotion engulfed me. I realized I, too, was cradled in the arms of the divine—safe, loved, and utterly protected. In that moment, I felt at home, embraced by God, Krishna. My worries dissolved, and I understood: *I belonged to God, and I had nothing to fear.*

Chanting and prayer helps us transcend our petty worries and gives us a connection to the universe beyond ourselves. Then, in that space of abundance, we are able to come back to our duties of this world with more effectiveness.

In our tradition, we also chant the *Hare Krishna* mantra in a musical ensemble, using various melodies and instruments such as hand cymbals, mrdanga, harmonium, and drums. This practice is called *sankirtan*, where *kirtan* refers to singing the glories of the Lord, and the prefix *san* signifies togetherness. During *sankirtan*, one devotee leads the chanting of the *Hare Krishna* mantra, and others respond in unison.

The musical element added to the chanting of God's Holy Names elevates one's spiritual experience to an entirely different level.

#2 Music, Mantras, and Spiritual Transformation

Three devout Muslims collaborated to create a masterpiece of Hindu devotional music. Mohammad Rafi sang the iconic semi-classical song, *"Man Tarpat Hari Darshan Ko Aaj"* (My mind yearns to see the Lord), set in the raga *Malkauns*. The music was composed by the legendary Naushad for the film *Baiju Bawra*, with lyrics penned by Shakeel Badayuni.

As Rafi completed the recording, the studio fell into a reverent silence, mesmerized by his melodic improvisation. His soulful rendition stirred deep spiritual emotions among those present. Babloo, the film's financer, was so moved that tears welled up in his eyes, and his body trembled with ecstasy. When he regained his composure, an unspoken realization hung in the air: they had just witnessed something transcendent, beyond the ordinary bounds of time and space.

Overwhelmed with gratitude, Babloo thanked Rafi profusely for the soothing and uplifting effect of his singing. Rafi, ever humble, credited Naushad for composing such a masterpiece. Naushad, in turn, ascribed the glory to Shakeel's profound lyrics. Shakeel, equally modest, acknowledged Rafi's unparalleled versatility in bringing the words to life. When the others turned to Rafi in awe, he simply bowed his head and remarked, "*Yeh raga Malkauns ki barkat hai*" (This is the blessing of raga *Malkauns*).

At the film's release, some critics questioned the inclusion of classical music in an era dominated by racy, commercial tracks. Naushad defended his choice, emphasizing that classical music is a vital part of India's cultural heritage. He also extolled the timeless beauty of raga *Malkauns*, recounting its legendary origins in the story of Goddess Parvati soothing Lord Shiva during his fierce *tandava* (dance of destruction).

Music is the soul of Indian traditions, transcending religious boundaries. When sound embodies divine love, it becomes a mantra—a sacred vibration that propels us toward spiritual awakening.

Mantra chanting is akin to the work of a sculptor, who chisels away excess stone to reveal the hidden masterpiece within. Practitioners of *Hare Krishna* meditation engage in various spiritual practices like hearing, chanting, deity worship, pilgrimage, celebrating festivals, and studying scriptures. These practices help peel away the layers of false identification that obscure the soul's true nature.

We often mistakenly define ourselves by temporary attributes—our gender, beauty, wealth, or social status. These external identities tether us to material consciousness, leading to frustration and overthinking. However, through mantra meditation, we gradually release these false layers, revealing our eternal identity as servants of God.

Chanting acts as a purification process. Just as rainwater becomes impure upon touching the earth, our souls are clouded by material attachments. Chanting the *Hare Krishna* mantra functions like a filter, scraping away these impurities.

A practitioner who chants daily, with focus and devotion, steadily disassociates from false identities and reconnects with their true spiritual self.

#3 Two Distinct Advantages of Prayer and Chanting

Prayer and chanting bring about two major transformations in a sincere practitioner:

1. **Increased tolerance:** The ability to endure provocations—both from the restless mind and the chaotic external world—significantly improves.
2. **Enhanced affection:** A deep love for Krishna naturally expands into affection for all living beings, recognizing others as children of the same loving God.

1. Increased tolerance (Training the mind through discipline)

Establishing a daily chanting practice in a dedicated space disciplines the mind. As you sit to chant for an hour or two, the mind invariably begins to wander. It tempts you to stop or distracts you with trivial urges like checking WhatsApp notifications. But as you persist, gently returning to the mantra each time, the mind's protests grow louder—urgent pleas, desperate screams—until it finally surrenders.

This is when the mind begins to resonate with the transcendental sound of the Lord's holy names. Gradually, this practice brings peace amidst the external world's chaos and the inner turbulence of one's thoughts. Chanting becomes an anchor, keeping you grounded, composed, and spiritually aligned.

As a teenager, I loved watching live cricket matches at Mumbai's iconic Wankhede Stadium. My father would often secure VIP passes for international games. Once, I received two passes for a much-anticipated match and invited a friend to join me.

This friend harbored a notorious hatred for Mumbai's local trains. He would complain incessantly about the overcrowded coaches, the jostling passengers, and the unpleasant odors. His tirades against the trains were so frequent that they had become a running joke in our college.

On the day of the match, however, his mood was different. Despite traveling the same route to the stadium, he beamed with joy and made no complaints. Surprised, I asked him about it. He tapped the VIP pass in his shirt pocket and said, "I spent the entire journey meditating on this ticket and the match I'm about to watch. The trains felt like paradise today!"

His perspective had shifted entirely because his mind was fixed on something higher—his excitement for the match. The chaos of the trains no longer bothered him.

A dedicated chanter of the Lord's holy names experiences a similar transformation. Daily meditation on Krishna fills the heart with a sense of belonging and love. This connection acts like my friend's VIP pass—it shields the practitioner from the disturbances of the external world. The nagging demands of the mind lose their grip, and overthinking becomes a relic of another life. The practitioner's happiness transcends the mind and senses, resting firmly in the spiritual realm.

2. Enhanced affection (Unity through chanting)

Beyond tolerance, chanting fosters a deep bond with all living beings. All life on this planet shares the same resources—air, water, earth—and follows the same universal laws of birth, death, aging, and disease. Regardless of our race, religion, or geography, we are all connected as parts of the same divine creation.

Chanting and prayer gradually reveal this truth, helping a practitioner see others as fellow children of God. It is reminiscent of the classic Bollywood trope where two brothers, separated in childhood, grow up unaware of their shared bond. Life's struggles take them down divergent paths, often pitting them against each other as adversaries. The predictable climax sees them on the verge of a fatal confrontation, only for one to notice a familiar birthmark on the other's arm. This discovery leads to an emotional revelation of their brotherhood. They drop their weapons, embrace each other, and begin a renewed, harmonious life together.

In much the same way, chanting and prayer unveil the shared "marks" of divinity within all living beings. These practices help us recognize that we are all children of the same loving God, interconnected at the deepest level. This realization emerges gradually for a sincere practitioner, but when it does, it transforms their outlook on life. Love, compassion and affection for others naturally blossom, dissolving the barriers of religious discord and jingoistic pride. Empathy replaces hostility, and cooperation becomes the guiding principle, fostering a world united by shared humanity and spiritual kinship.

ISKCON provides a vibrant example of this transformation. When I began visiting the ISKCON temple in Mumbai, I was struck by the diversity of people participating in *kirtan*. Africans and Americans danced joyfully together; a Pashtun man from Pakistan donned traditional attire and chanted *Hare Krishna*, while Punjabis and South Indian Brahmins worked hand in hand to organize events.

In this spiritual space, external differences dissolved. What united them was their shared connection to Krishna, cultivated through prayer and chanting. This sense of unity and affection for others is a natural by-product of sincere spiritual practice, making the world a happier place.

#4 Uniting Strange Worlds by Chanting Holy Names

What are the odds of an elderly Indian Swami, speaking with a Bengali accent, embarking on a cargo ship to the United States, without money or a fixed place to stay, and inspiring drug-affected hippies to embrace a life of God-consciousness? Yet Srila Prabhupada accomplished just that. Not only did he transform the countercultural youth of 1960s America but he also led them to a life free of intoxication, illicit sex, meat-eating, and gambling—anchored in the chanting of God's holy names.

Starting from a humble storefront on 26 Second Avenue in New York City, Srila Prabhupada began his mission with *kirtans*—chanting and dancing to the *Hare Krishna* mantra. His small group of followers was skeptical when he asked them to take *kirtans* to Washington Square Park. "That's just not done in America," they protested, fearing ridicule. But Srila Prabhupada, with his characteristic warmth and confidence, encouraged them to trust him.

The devotees reluctantly complied, braving jeers and curious stares as they made their way to the park. At first, their *kirtan*—marked by devotional attire, cymbals, and drums—seemed bizarre to onlookers. Yet as Srila Prabhupada began to sing, his energy and faith drew people in. Slowly, the rhythmic mantra and beats inspired onlookers to join the singing and dancing. For over two hours, the park resonated with the *Hare Krishna* mantra, breaking the American silence, as Srila Prabhupada had envisioned.

When the group returned to the storefront temple that evening, they were ecstatic. They told Srila Prabhupada that they should organize such *kirtans* every week. With a gentle smile, he corrected them: "Every day."

Five years later, Srila Prabhupada brought his American disciples to Surat, Gujarat. In a reversal of roles, his Western devotees led rousing *kirtans* through the streets, drawing thousands of enthusiastic locals to join. Srila Prabhupada fondly called these disciples his "dancing white elephants," marveling at how the Holy Names had united people across cultures. Similar scenes played out in Mumbai, Delhi, Kolkata, Montreal, and London.

One of the movement's most notable supporters was George Harrison of The Beatles. Deeply moved by Srila Prabhupada and the chanting of *Hare Krishna*, Harrison sponsored a record, donated a large estate to ISKCON, helped finance the publication of *Krishna: The Supreme*

Personality of Godhead, and even penned its foreword. His endorsement brought the mantra to a global stage, helping Srila Prabhupada's vision of spreading the Holy Names to "every town and village" take root.

Srila Prabhupada described chanting as more than just a sound—it was a divine vibration. Quoting ancient scriptures, he explained, *"The sound of Hare Krishna transcends the bodily, mental, and intellectual spheres and touches the very soul."* He emphasized that chanting, done with love and devotion, purifies the heart and connects the practitioner directly with God.

Srila Prabhupada's unwavering faith in the potency of chanting and his tireless efforts to share this gift were the keys to his success. He inspired his followers to see *kirtan* not as a mere performance but as an act of devotion capable of uniting hearts, transcending boundaries, and elevating consciousness.

His life's work transformed both East and West, proving that even the strangest of worlds could be united under the banner of divine love and the sacred vibration of the Holy Names.

#5 Radhanath Swami Receives the Holy Names

In the serene, sacred town of Rishikesh, nestled along the Ganges, a 19-year-old seeker named Richard Slavin embarked on a spiritual journey. Having left behind the comforts of America, Richard hitchhiked across Europe and Asia in search of God. Now, in this ancient pilgrimage site, where saints and sages have meditated for centuries, he immersed himself in deep meditation.

For over a month, Richard sustained himself solely on a single carrot and water from the Ganges. From sunrise to sunset, he sat on a rock by the river, meditating on the ceaseless song of the sacred Ganges. The river's powerful yet gentle flow resonated with the cosmic sound of *Om,* reverberating through the valley.

One day, amidst this spiritual stillness, Richard heard a melody that seemed to rise from the very heart of Mother Ganges—the *Hare Krishna maha-mantra*:

Hare Krishna Hare Krishna
Krishna Krishna Hare Hare
Hare Rama Hare Rama
Rama Rama Hare Hare

In his autobiography, *The Journey Home,* Radhanath Swami recounts this transformative moment. Though he had never heard the mantra before, its sacred sound resonated deeply within him. "Through the song of the river, I felt God had whispered this beautiful mantra into my ears," he reflects. The experience was unlike anything he had ever encountered. "No intoxication on earth could come close to the bliss of the *Hare Krishna* mantra," he says.

Some weeks later, while battling the powerful currents of the Ganges and facing the prospect of drowning, Richard once again heard the mantra resounding in his heart. Its sacred sound filled him with an unshakable peace that transcended fear, guiding him through the perilous moment.

Richard's spiritual journey eventually led him to Srila

Prabhupada, the founder of the International Society for Krishna Consciousness (ISKCON), whom he accepted as his spiritual master. Under Srila Prabhupada's guidance, he learned the systematic practice of chanting the *Hare Krishna* mantra. What began as an unexplainable attraction to the mantra on the banks of the Ganges was now fortified by a deep understanding of its spiritual significance, rooted in centuries-old Vedic tradition.

Today, as Radhanath Swami, he continues to share the transformative power of the Holy Names, spreading the joy and wisdom he first encountered as a young seeker in the lap of Mother Ganges.

#6 The Six Rules of Chanting

While the experiences of Srila Prabhupada, Radhanath Swami, and other advanced spiritualists with chanting are awe-inspiring, many others encounter more modest realizations. In fact, numerous practitioners admit that chanting can be challenging. They often face moments of doubt and frustration, questioning why their sincere efforts do not produce the promised results.

For seekers on the path of Bhakti-Yoga, the six rules of chanting can illuminate the way. These guidelines, originally outlined over five hundred years ago by Srila Sanatana Goswami in his *Sri Hari-Bhakti-Vilasa,* offer a systematic approach to perfecting the chanting of the *Hare Krishna maha-mantra*. Following even one or two of these rules can bring tangible spiritual benefits.

Rule 1: Bring the mind back (*Manah samskaranam*)

When chanting the *Hare Krishna* mantra, the mind often wanders. This is a natural tendency, not a flaw. Lord Krishna addresses this in the *Bhagavad Gita* (6.26):

> *"From wherever the mind wanders due to its flickering and unsteady nature, one must certainly withdraw it and bring it back under the control of the self."*

To successfully practice this rule, one needs to cultivate honesty and humility. Accepting our fallible nature and recognizing our limitations in accessing higher stages of realization allows us to move forward gradually and steadily in our practices.

There are several practical ways to bring the wandering mind back during meditation. One friend of mine places a printed *Hare Krishna* mantra in front of him while chanting. Fixing his gaze on the syllables helps him maintain focus on the sound. Another friend uses a placard with the question: "Where are you, oh mind? Please come back to the sound of the Holy Names!" This gentle reminder helps redirect his attention to the mantra. Such simple strategies can effectively refocus the mind on the Holy Names.

In the *Hare Krishna* tradition, the essence of meditation lies in listening attentively to the sound of the mantra. When the mind inevitably drifts, the key is to return to the sound without judgment or frustration. The real issue is not that the mind wanders—it is whether we are willing to come back to the Holy Names when we notice it happening.

Each return to the mantra demonstrates our sincerity and commitment. During a two-hour session, I sometimes realize after ninety minutes that my mind has been elsewhere. At that moment, I face a choice: to return to the practice or abandon the effort. Often, the mind tries to discourage us, whispering, *"You have already wasted so much time. What is the point now?"* Choosing to return in those moments is an act of spiritual redemption and a reclaiming of lost ground.

Ultimately, spiritual advancement comes not from achieving perfect control over the mind or constant remembrance of God but from our repeated willingness to turn back to Krishna. This willingness to return, despite distractions, reflects the sincerity of our devotion and helps us progress on the path of spiritual realization.

Rule 2: Cleanliness (*Saucham*)

Saucham is not merely a technique of chanting; it is a way of life—a culture of cleanliness both external and internal. Externally, we may take a bath once or twice a day to cleanse the body. Internally, we must cultivate purity by consciously choosing positive and uplifting thoughts to bathe our minds.

In today's world, we value physical cleanliness—drinking bottled water, eating organic food, and being mindful of what we consume. However, just as we care for the cleanliness of our body, it is equally important to safeguard the purity of our consciousness. We violate the principle of *saucham* when we expose ourselves to content that fills the mind with desires rooted in passion and ignorance, often found on the internet or social media.

When we sit to chant, our past impressions surface, often playing out like movies on the screen of the mind. A sincere practitioner takes care to filter what they allow into their consciousness, knowing that these inputs influence their inner world. Many people are vigilant about what they eat, but do we exercise the same caution with the subject we consume through our social media feeds, news, and online interactions?

Every interface with the world leaves an imprint on the subconscious, stored for future retrieval. By carefully choosing what we allow into our minds in the present, we lay the foundation for a healthy, spiritually awakened future. Internal cleanliness is as essential as external hygiene, for it shapes the quality of our thoughts, emotions, and ultimately, our spiritual practice.

Rule 3: Silence (*Maunam*)

Connected to cleanliness is the principle of silence. When we engage in unnecessary talk, especially on subjects that have no bearing on our emotional or spiritual well-being, we drift further away from a state of peaceful living.

Consider this: does it really matter which celebrity is dating whom or who will win the presidential election? Are our own challenges not enough that we feel compelled to take on the problems of the world as well? By eliminating the clutter of mundane chatter, we create space to access a deeper reality within ourselves. In contrast, spiritual discussions have the opposite effect—they draw us closer to the divine reality of Krishna.

During chanting, if we text a friend, take a phone call, or multitask in any way, we disrupt the "silence" that chanting requires. This time is meant to be an exclusive meeting with God, an opportunity to deepen our relationship with Krishna. Dividing our attention undermines this sacred connection.

Silence also encompasses integrity in speech—not speaking harmfully about others or ourselves. It includes listening to spiritual discourses from sincere practitioners with an open and attentive mind. In conversations, we often wait for our turn to speak, rather than genuinely listening. Overcoming this tendency to talk, and instead practicing *maunam*—the discipline of attentive listening to spiritual topics without the urge to respond or outsmart—demonstrates a noble character and inner strength.

Moreover, silence conserves energy, which can then be channeled into chanting the Holy Names of Krishna. Over the years, I have adopted a rule during my travels: I give a maximum of one lecture per day, even when there is pressure to deliver multiple talks. I established this boundary because I noticed that excessive social interaction left me drained the following morning, affecting the quality of my chanting. When I overexerted myself, my *japa* would feel like a task to "finish" rather than a heartfelt meditation to "complete." Instead of focusing on Krishna on the chanting beads, I found myself overly concerned with the counter beads used to count the sixteen rounds that I chant on my beads.

By limiting my social exchanges, I preserve the energy needed for focused spiritual practice. Silence, when practiced with care, becomes a powerful ally in our journey toward spiritual advancement.

Rule 4: Meditate on the meaning of the mantra (*Mantrartha chintanam*)

The *Hare Krishna* mantra translates as: "Oh Mother Hara, Oh Lord Krishna, Oh Lord Rama, please engage me in Your service." Chanting, therefore, is a heartfelt call for service. If, as we vibrate the syllables of the mantra with our lips, we simultaneously meditate on its meaning, we can uncover deeper layers of spiritual connection.

While the first rule of chanting emphasizes bringing the wandering mind back to the sound of the Holy Names, it is equally, if not more, important to meditate on the mantra's meaning. Without this meditation, we risk becoming mind-controlling yogis rather than seekers of a loving relationship with Krishna. The essence of Bhakti-Yoga lies in fostering this relationship, not merely regulating the mind. Pulling the mind back to the mantra is significant, but the intention behind that action carries greater weight.

By meditating on the mantra's meaning, we align our chanting with the positive intention of seeking a relationship with Krishna. This shifts our focus from ritualistic chanting or intellectual preaching to true self-transformation. It helps us approach the Lord with a spirit of service, rather than for personal gains or benefits. This heartfelt meditation allows us to connect with Krishna in the realm of love.

Many mistakenly believe that simply completing the external formalities of chanting will bring spiritual advancement. However, without delving into the mantra's meaning, our experience becomes superficial—like trying to taste honey by licking the outside of the jar. The Holy Names are as sweet as honey, but their essence remains inaccessible to those who focus only on outward customs. True progress comes when we internalize the meaning, transforming our chanting into a heartfelt dialogue with Krishna.

The dangers of ritualistic chanting are vividly captured in a folktale from Central India:

One day, a lost traveler found himself wandering in a dense and desolate forest, unsure of how to find his way out. Just as despair began to set in, he encountered a sage who, feeling compassion for the man, offered him a solution. "Oh young man, I have a horse that can sprint through this jungle at lightning speed, but you must chant the mantra, 'Thank God,' to make it run faster. When you reach the outskirts of the forest, you will need to chant another mantra to stop the horse: 'Please save me.' If you fail to chant this, the horse will not stop."

The young man quickly mounted the stallion, and commanded, 'Thank God' and the horse sped like a raging wind. Even as the elderly monk wished to revise the chanting, the young man was in no mood to waste time. He instantly disappeared out of sight like an arrow shot from a bow.

Before long, the man had made it out of the forbidden woods, but when he wished to stop the horse, he found that it wouldn't slow down. "Stop!" he shouted, but the horse only sped faster. Panicked, the man tried again, "Stop!" but the horse continued to race ahead. Realizing he had forgotten the second mantra, the only one he remembered was "Thank God," and the more he chanted it, the faster the horse ran. Soon, the horse was heading straight for a mountain. The man desperately wanted it to stop, but the animal was unstoppable.

In a panic, just as the horse reached the cliff's edge, the man remembered the correct mantra and shouted, "Please save me." Instantly, the horse came to a screeching halt, right on the edge of the mountain. The young man, trembling with relief, let out a sigh of gratitude and exclaimed, "Thank God!"

The danger of chanting mechanically, without real attention or emotion, is that it leads to a superficial experience, detached from the deeper meaning and connection to the divine. Although the sound itself is purifying and would burn negativities from our heart, like fire would burn regardless of your knowledge of its properties, still, true chanting requires the investment of emotions and a sincere connection to the Lord. And this would happen when we focus on the meaning of the mantra, not just the repetition of its sounds.

Rule 5: Patience (*Avyagratva*)

The first time I read this rule, which essentially means "don't rush the practice," it was a moment of epiphany for me. The greatest challenge for many unfulfilled spiritual seekers is ticking off all the boxes. We become so focused on doing things correctly that we forget to do the right things. We emphasize efficiency over effectiveness. We want to complete all our commitments as quickly as possible, not realizing that there is so much more to spiritual life than simply fulfilling duties and obligations. Krishna consciousness is about offering our heart to Krishna—it is about calling out to the Lord in love. And love is not a hurried practice; it is an experience of being fully present in the moment.

When we chant at a natural pace, with the desire to connect with God, we make our practice personal. It is unloving to rush through *japa* meditation with the sole intention of finishing it quickly. It is like being with someone who is eager to end the conversation just to move on to the next thing. Would you feel cherished or humiliated in such a scenario? Similarly, when we chant in a mood of "getting it done" as a mere ritual, Krishna may feel unloved and might leave us even before we finish our meeting with Him. True devotion requires that we offer our full attention and heart, rather than rushing to complete a task.

Rule 6: Steadfastness (*Anirveda*)

Often, the results of chanting don't come immediately. During such times, it is essential to continue without losing hope.

We live in an era where the mere push of a button gives us instant access to information and conveniences from across the globe. If we are not immediately stimulated, we tend to abandon the pursuit. However, chanting doesn't offer instant gratification—it is meant for connection and satisfaction. There is a world of difference between stimulation and satisfaction. Chanting is not a dopamine-inducing practice; it is meant to help us access a deeper connection with Krishna.

For rewards that are truly satisfying, one must remain steadfast and persistent in the practice. To stay steady even when the results are not immediately visible requires both faith and humility.

Milo, a six-time Olympic champion from ancient Greece, serves as an inspiring example. One day, he walked into a packed stadium carrying a four-year-old bull on his shoulders. To truly grasp the significance, imagine a man carrying a premium hatchback car, weighing a thousand kilograms on his back. That's the feat Milo achieved in 500 B.C.

However, what led to this spectacular moment is just as important. A few years before this, Milo had seen a calf born near his home. He picked it up, carried it a few miles, and then repeated the feat every day. As the calf grew, so did Milo's strength. Over time, his consistent efforts allowed him to carry not a 25-kg calf, but a thousand-kg bull.

Milo's story illustrates three key steps:

1. **Humble:** Start small.
2. **Steady:** Do it daily.
3. **Improve:** Make small, regular progress.

By following these steps, we, too, can build our spiritual strength and progress steadily, even when the results are not immediately visible.

#7 The Golden Rule to Follow the Six Rules

If Milo had attempted to lift a full-sized bull on his first day, what chance would he have had for success? None! He started humbly, building his strength gradually. However, as a champion, when he was carrying a bull around, he forgot the importance of remaining small. A crucial but often overlooked truth is that humility is essential, even when the world perceives you as great. If we allow our fame or success to outgrow our humility, it can very well become our undoing.

Success, especially when it elevates us to the top, can be fleeting. The earth revolves in a day, after all, and so too can our achievements fade. Milo, unfortunately, took his glory too seriously and allowed pride to creep in. He began showing off his strength, and one day, while in the forest, he saw a crack in a tree and violently wrenched it out. But luck was not on his side—his hands became trapped as the cleft closed around them. Unable to escape, he was soon attacked by a pack of wolves and met a tragic end.

This is a reflection of life—it is always ready to humble us. It is far better to choose humility voluntarily than to wait for the material world to humble us through its relentless forces. Milo was successful, but because his mind was filled with thoughts of his own greatness, he became spiritually empty.

We chant daily, often for decades, and humbly wait for the Lord to reciprocate with our sincerity. Humility allows us to maintain the right relationship with God, regardless of the external successes or failures we encounter.

Humility is not merely a skill or technique—it is the essence of a *Hare Krishna* devotee's life. A sincere spiritualist genuinely seeks to respect others and practices tolerance in challenging situations.

A Bhakti-Yoga practitioner does not aim to control his mind like a yogi. Rather, he strives to please Krishna, and for the sake of Krishna's service, he regulates his mind and places his life in the Lord's hands. The definition of success for a Bhakti yogi is different from that of other yogis or mystics. We do not seek to "achieve" anything; instead, we seek to "receive" the Lord's blessings.

To win the Lord's favor, which empowers us to serve Him, we practice all disciplines sincerely. We rise early, chant, and serve—all with the intention to please God. Even when life feels burdensome, a devotee marches forward quietly, regardless of personal feelings. A devotee thinks, "I am a servant of Krishna. Even if I feel lazy or unenthusiastic, I will chant my rounds today because Krishna is pleased. My happiness is secondary to Krishna's satisfaction."

#8 Going Deeper Into *Hare Krishna* Chanting

Cultivating this mood is challenging for one who believes that spiritual life is about 'my' happiness. Bhakti-Yoga challenges our conventional idea of happiness and teaches us that the Lord is the root of the cosmic tree. If we water the root, the branches and twigs also flourish. If I decorate my face, my reflection in the mirror will appear beautiful. If I nourish my stomach, my hands and legs will be sustained. Similarly, if I seek to please my beloved Lord, I will find true contentment.

This paradigm keeps us grounded in spiritual consciousness. Humility naturally develops when one serves God as a reality higher than themselves. This mood softens the heart and helps a practitioner perceive the Lord's presence always.

I witnessed this unconventional paradigm in action when I joined the monastery. Balarama Dasa, a dear friend, taught me through his example the sacred lesson of humility.

Balarama would often feel sleepy every morning. Whenever he sat down to chant, his eyes would droop, and his neck would fall forward. I would gently wake him, and he'd vigorously shake his head, open his eyes, and resume chanting loudly.

We chant our morning *japa*, a form of quiet, private meditation, in a circle of six to seven devotees. Each member focuses on their own chanting, and the circular seating arrangement helps us draw strength from one another and encourage each other. If one of us becomes sleepy, another will gently pat them on the lap to bring them back to the practice. During this two-hour *japa* meditation before sunrise, many circles form in the temple hall. This shared commitment to *sadhana*—spiritual practice of hearing, chanting, *kirtans*—lasts for five hours each morning and helps the monks stay strong and focused throughout the day.

Balarama was sincere, but throughout the morning program, he struggled to stay awake. During the 5 a.m. *kirtan*, when we all stood with palms folded in supplication as one of us led the chants, Balarama would often doze off, even while standing. Then, he'd pull himself up and chant with the others. His biggest challenge, however, came during the two hours of *japa* meditation. Each mantra felt like a drag for him. He would repeatedly lurch forward while moving his beads, seated in the circle. Then he'd sway from left to right, chanting with great effort.

I sat next to him and almost always had to wake him up repeatedly during each *japa* session. I never fell asleep myself and sat upright throughout the entire two-hour session, chanting as attentively as possible. I felt sorry for Balarama and thought I was helping him progress in his spiritual life.

Subconsciously, though, I allowed false pride to creep in. I began to feel superior to him as a devotee because I never dozed off during the morning program. I even kept a sadhana card, a daily tracker of my spiritual activities. It had columns for how much scripture I studied, the services I rendered, and so on. One column was dedicated to scoring my chanting. If I felt I had chanted attentively, I'd give myself a score of nine out of ten. If my *japa* session was distracted, the score would naturally go down. I kept this score daily, attempting to monitor and record my spiritual progress.

One evening, I returned late after a college program and had only three hours of rest that night. During the morning *japa* session, I began to feel drowsy and struggled to stay awake, let alone chant attentively. Meanwhile, my partner Balarama's situation was no different—his struggle was all too familiar, and today, I was right there with him. As we both fought hard to keep our minds awake, my body ached, and I couldn't sit still any longer. I stood up and began pacing up and down while chanting, but still, sleep overtook every cell of my body.

I lazily dragged myself to the medical facility in the ashram, a room with four cozy beds reserved exclusively for devotees recovering from sickness. When I entered, I saw a couple of beds were unoccupied, and without hesitation, I jumped into one. Two hours passed in deep sleep, and around 8.30 a.m., I woke up with a start. Realizing I had missed my duties during the morning program, I quickly washed my face and rushed to the temple hall. The morning class was in session, and everything seemed normal. The speaker was discussing the *Śrīmad-Bhāgavatam,* an ancient scripture, and the temple hall was half-filled with monks and guests attending the class.

I found a place in the middle of the hall and sat quietly, now feeling fresh and wide awake after my rest. Suddenly, I saw a familiar sight—Balarama was seated next to me, looking miserable. He could barely keep his eyes open. He rose from his seat and stood at the side of the hall, trying his best to stay attentive. His body kept reeling forward, as though it might fall to the ground. I kept staring at him, and although this wasn't anything unusual, suddenly a realization dawned on me.

In that moment, I felt humbled and inspired by my friend. He struggled every day but never gave up the fight. I had felt sleepy just once and given in to my body and mind's demands. But here was Balarama, continuously struggling—his determination to stay awake and grasp every word the speaker said was a testament to his own glory, to his sincerity in practicing spiritual discipline. I felt ashamed for having given up so easily and went up to him to congratulate and thank him for inspiring me.

Before I could say anything, he grasped my hand and said, "Please pray for me, my dear friend. I am so pathetic. I have no taste for chanting or hearing the Lord's glories, so I fall asleep all the time. But when devotees like you pray for me, I have some hope." I fell silent for a moment and then humbly pointed out how he had persisted in his struggle without giving up. I asked him what kept him going despite his body and mind's protests.

With a humble smile, he replied, "I have no other hope. This is the only way I can show my sincerity to Krishna."

That night, as I pulled out my *sadhana* tracker, another realization hit me hard: "My monitoring of spiritual practice is different from the way the Lord keeps track of my progress." Even as I give myself a score of nine out of ten, Krishna pulls out the original *sadhana* tracker that He holds with Him. He may dismiss my inflated self-assessment and instead give me a score of just one. On the other hand, my friend Balarama may consider himself mediocre and score himself as a one, but Krishna, seeing his authenticity and humility, may give him a perfect score of ten out of ten.

How the Lord sees us is vastly different from how we see

our spiritual lives. We focus on the externals, but the Lord looks at our intention, sincerity, and aspirations.

#9 Prayer at Three Levels (*Vaikari, Madhyama,* and *Pasyanti*)

Our aspiration is what the Lord sees as we attempt to pray. The path of Bhakti-Yoga recognizes sound and prayer at three distinct levels.

At the lowest level, prayer is words. In Sanskrit, this is called *vaikari*—sound in its manifest form as words. For example, you might say to your spouse, "I am going to the temple." Once spoken, these words become *vaikari*, the tangible form of sound.

Before speaking those words, you may have thought to yourself, "I need to go to the temple." This thought carries energy and is a form of sound, though subtle and unspoken. This is called *madhyama*. There is a significant difference between thinking, "He is a proud rascal" and actually saying it aloud. Both are sounds, but one exists as a thought form, while the other is manifest as words.

When we chant *Hare Krishna*, even if mindlessly, we are connecting to God at the level of manifest sound—*vaikari*. The mantra expresses our desire to serve, yet we may be disconnected from its meaning. In such cases, we are only producing the external sound of *Hare Krishna*. Bhakti-Yoga teaches us to go beyond the sound and enter the space of the mantra's meaning (*madhyama*).

The next level is the sound of feelings and aspirations, also known as *pasyanti*. Before speaking the words or even having a thought of going to temple, there may be a deep, wordless feeling or wave of remembrance, like a strong sense of shelter or connection to the temple. This is the subtlest form of sound, existing as an unspoken wave in the consciousness, difficult to capture but real nevertheless.

Similarly, for an advanced chanter of *Hare Krishna*, merely picking up their beads can evoke a feeling of protection and a flood of belonging in the heart.

The three levels of prayer are:

1. **Words** – *Vaikari*
2. **Thoughts** – *Madhyama*
3. **Aspiration or feelings** – *Pasyanti*

To illustrate further: When you hear the word "mother," a tribal person from the jungle who doesn't understand English may only hear the sound of the word, which means nothing to him—this is *vaikari*. However, if you understand the language, the word "mother" might trigger a thought, like, "I hope my mother is all right"—this is *madhyama*. As you think of your mother, a deep feeling of love and bonding may rise in your heart, like a wave of emotion—this is *pasyanti*.

A lot of chanting and prayer is performed externally, like a ritual—at the *vaikari* stage. A few of us invest thoughts into our prayer (*madhyama*). And yet, very few discover the deeper connection where emotions arise spontaneously, causing tears of affection as we hear the Lord's sweet Holy Names (*pasyanti*).

When I first attended an ISKCON program, the *kirtan* was sung to a familiar Bollywood melody. I hummed along, often excited when different singers performed the *kirtan* in catchy tunes. It was all external. I was chanting and connecting to the Lord at the *vaikari* level. My prayers were superficial, focused only on the words or manifest sound.

Slowly, I began to learn the meaning of the mantra and shifted my focus to my thoughts as I externally vibrated the mantra on my lips. Even as I chanted, seated amidst a congregation of over a thousand people, I silently prayed, "Oh Mother Radha, Oh Krishna, please allow me to serve You and Your devotees." This was *madhyama*, a subtler connection with the Lord through thought.

With time and practice, I started to connect to God on the level of feelings—*pasyanti*. Sometimes, a deep sense of shelter would arise as a wave in my heart when I heard the chanting of *Hare Krishna*. Srila Prabhupada described chanting *Hare Krishna* as being like the crying of a child for her mother. The child doesn't think or speak eloquently; she simply feels that the world is a dreary void without her mother. She helplessly calls out to her mother. The feeling that drives the child to seek shelter is the same feeling we seek as devotees of Krishna. We long to feel that love, and that deep desire and eagerness to receive Krishna's love is what attracts His grace upon us. This yearning is what qualifies us to attract His attention.

Srila Prabhupada writes in the *Nectar of Devotion* (Chapter 9):

> *"In other words, one should learn how to cry for the Lord. One should learn this small technique, and he should be very eager and actually cry to become engaged in some particular type of service. ... And such tears are the price for the highest perfection. If one develops this excessive eagerness for meeting and serving*

the Lord in a particular way, this is the price to enter into the kingdom of God. Otherwise, there is no material calculation for the value of the ticket by which one can enter the kingdom of God. The only price for such entrance is this desire and great eagerness."

As beginners on the path of Bhakti-Yoga, we first learn to pray with words. Slowly, we begin to invest our thoughts, and with practice, feelings develop. These spiritual feelings are the beautiful, blossomed flowers of Bhakti-Yoga that arise in our consciousness.

To reach these advanced stages, we simply need to develop a sincere attitude of service.

#10 Sincerity – The Most Important Ingredient

Those who overthink their worries often develop cynical and negative feelings. Prayer, on the other hand, is a conscious choice to change the words we speak to ourselves. When *Hare Krishna* devotees consciously choose thoughts of service and purer aspirations, their inner mindset shifts, effectively neutralizing the addiction to overthinking.

You may protest, "But I can't artificially pray to serve when, in truth, I desire to enjoy." You might say out loud and clearly that you want to serve (*vaikari*) and even chant repeatedly in your mind, "I want to serve" (*madhyama*). Yet, deep within, you may still harbor a desire for carnal pleasures and wish to stay away from God (*pasyanti*). Despite years of positive self-talk, you may feel no real connection with God.

Does this make you a hypocrite?

No! This is where sincerity comes into play.

Sincerity means two things: *knowing where you are* and *not remaining where you are*. The first part is to honestly acknowledge your current level of consciousness and make peace with it. Sincerity is about living a non-pretentious life, grounded in honesty. The second aspect of sincerity is to strive to rise above your limitations and move forward. This is called aspiration.

Vijay's journey of sincerity

Vijay was a reticent, hard-working young man when he joined the ashram. He quickly won hearts with his service attitude and quiet demeanor. One day, he was asked to give the morning class. His immediate response was, "No way!" He refused, citing his lack of ability to make coherent presentations. However, the program in-charge insisted, and Vijay, though hesitant, surrendered to the request and spoke to the class in a monotone voice. There was no emotion, enthusiasm, or emphasis in his delivery. Yet, when he finished, the entire ashram gathered around him in joy. They appreciated his class, some recalling striking points, while others highlighted his mood of surrender and devotion. The atmosphere in the temple was festive.

Unfazed by the praise and unassuming as ever, Vijay silently continued with his other duties for the day. Life went on as usual for him, until a month later when he was once again asked to give a class. Each time he spoke, people were touched and inspired. It didn't take long for me to realize his secret. It was his purity of intention and sincerity of service that won hearts; the style of speech was a minor detail. He didn't try to be something he was not, yet he fully embraced the opportunity to serve and surrendered to the order of service. This combination of sincerity and humility helped him win the hearts of devotees in the community.

Vijay's speech (*vaikari*) may have seemed simple, but what truly mattered was the thought process he cultivated (*madhyama*) and his subconscious desire to serve (*pasyanti*). As the iconic American philosopher Ralph Waldo Emerson once said, "What you do and who you are speaks so loud that I cannot hear what you say." Sincerity cannot be hidden or masked by words; it is as clear as the midday sun. And it captures hearts. Sincerity and love are palpable in the energy they exude.

In a track and field event for mentally handicapped athletes in Spokane, Washington, in 1976, one of the contestants slipped, tumbled on the asphalt, and began to cry. Two other athletes, also with Down syndrome, heard him fall and wail. They turned back, looked at him expressionlessly at first, then picked him up. The three of them linked arms and crossed the finish line together, smiling and rejoicing.

That evening, two individuals whom many might call "challenged" or "sick" taught us a powerful lesson in humanness through their unspoken language of love and care—*pasyanti* speech. Meanwhile, the so-called "smart" and "heroic" individuals of this world often fail to deliver the lessons in kindness and sincerity that these athletes with disabilities imparted.

#11 Five Ways We Develop Our Sincerity

There are many ways to show our sincerity in our spiritual practice. Here, we explore five key ways I have learned from my guru, His Holiness Radhanath Swami, and from His Divine Grace, Srila A.C. Bhaktivedanta Swami Srila Prabhupada.

1. Chanting early morning to catch god's attention

Chanting *Hare Krishna* is most effective when performed during the early hours of the day. These early hours are filled with *sattva*, the energy of purity and goodness. You'll notice that many spiritual practitioners perform their most important practices just as the sun begins to rise. While the world is still asleep, a spiritualist remains awake to absorb these higher vibrations of *sattva*.

In traditional Vedic temples and Bhakti-Yoga centers, the period just before sunrise is considered sacred—God's time to wake up and reciprocate with the heartfelt prayers of His devotees. It is during these early hours that devotees engage in devotional songs, called *kirtans*, which are sung with great love and devotion.

A serious Bhakti-Yoga practitioner rises early, chants *Hare Krishna*, and aligns themselves with this powerful time of grace. The intention is to capture God's attention and receive His abundant mercy.

While God is merciful at all times, the early morning hours offer a special opportunity. During this time, the atmosphere is more peaceful, with fewer distractions of daily life. A businessman may be industrious throughout the year but can take advantage of special occasions, like Diwali or Christmas, when there are unique opportunities for prosperity. Similarly, the early morning is an "opportunist's delight" for a sincere practitioner, allowing them to tap into the rich, positive vibrations that permeate the ether at that time.

Nature is governed by three primary energies: goodness (*sattva*), passion (*rajas*), and ignorance (*tamas*). The energy of *sattva* predominates in the early morning, making it easier for a practitioner to calm the mind and enter a peaceful state of existence. As the day progresses, the mind becomes increasingly occupied with the demands of various tasks, pulling our attention away from spiritual practices. By sunset, *tamas* sets in, which is why traditional wisdom suggests that this is the time for rest. Attempting serious spiritual practices after sunset becomes more difficult as the mind is tired from the day's exertions, and the effort required to meditate intensifies as the night goes on. We will study *sattva* in greater detail in the last chapter of this book.

What if you're used to waking up well after 9 a.m.? Is there still hope of reaping the spiritual benefits that come from early morning Bhakti-Yoga practice?

Bhakti-Yoga is a gradual process of transformation that involves cultivating positive and desirable habits. If you currently wake up late, you can start by gradually shifting your wake-up time. For example, begin by waking up at 8.30 a.m. After a week of consistency, you can shift to 8 a.m., and so on. By making small half-hour adjustments, you can eventually reach a time that allows you to rise just before sunrise. Commit to this early morning practice for three months, and you will begin to notice a significant shift in your consciousness. The proof, as they say, is in the experience.

2. Becoming an expert gardener

Lord Chaitanya Mahaprabhu, who inaugurated the *Hare Krishna* chanting movement over five hundred fifty years ago, compared a *Hare Krishna* yogi to a gardener.

Love for Krishna is likened to a beautiful plant that grows when the seed of devotional service is planted in the heart by genuine devotees of Krishna. The very fact that some of us are regularly chanting *Hare Krishna* means we have been fortunate enough to receive this seed of devotional service. It is now our responsibility to water that seed with consistent and disciplined chanting.

However, as we water the seed of devotional service, we must also be cautious not to allow weeds to grow in our consciousness. Any motive or desire that is not aligned with serving Krishna is considered a weed. This includes negative tendencies such as envy, lust, pride, anger, and other impurities that are deeply rooted in the heart. Just as a plant grows when watered, so do these weeds silently grow as we continue our practice of chanting *Hare Krishna*. If we're not vigilant in removing them, they can eventually destroy the growth of the devotional plant.

A true chanter of *Hare Krishna*, like an intelligent gardener, is introspective and regularly examines their motives and aspirations. We must diligently rid our hearts of these weeds and nurture pure aspirations while chanting the Holy Names.

As we progress in our practice of devotional service, many side benefits can arise, such as respect, love, honor, and recognition in the community of devotees. This is especially true as we become more senior in the community. These offerings of position and praise can become potential weeds if we're not careful. The trap is when we start to accept these honors as something we deserve, or when we begin to crave and hanker for admiration and adoration. At that point, we allow these weeds to choke the growth of our devotion and obstruct the purity of our chanting.

A gardener doesn't simply water the plants; he also spends time checking for weeds. Similarly, a *Hare Krishna* devotee is not content merely to finish his prescribed rounds and then go about the rest of his day. He remains vigilant, aware of the potential for being honored or seeking praise. In the *Hare Krishna* tradition, devotees address one another as *prabhu* (master) and view themselves as servants. Radhanath Swami warns that, over time, hearing others call us *prabhu* may cause us to mistakenly accept the position of a master. "If someone calls us *prabhu* (master), we should think, 'This person is so advanced that they can see even me as *prabhu*'; we shouldn't think, 'Everyone is calling me *prabhu*, it must be true'."

To truly experience the benefits of chanting *Hare Krishna*, devotees must cultivate the mood of being a servant of God and others. Even if a devotee is given a senior position, he should accept it as an opportunity to increase his service to Krishna. This humble approach creates a favorable environment for sincere chanting of the Holy Names.

The scriptures recount a historical incident involving Shri Madhavendra Puri, a devout chanter who lived in Vrindavan, India. Once, while in Remuna, Orissa, an extraordinary event occurred in which the Lord, in His deity form, stole a pot of sweet rice for Madhavendra Puri (refer to the last section of the previous chapter). However, upon realizing that the townspeople might soon honor him for having inspired such a sweet pastime by the Lord, Madhavendra Puri immediately feared the attention. In the middle of the night, he fled the town, desperately wanting to avoid any praise or recognition. This story exemplifies the mood of a sincere chanter: one who seeks to avoid honor or respect and is simply happy to glorify Krishna through chanting the Holy Names and recounting the Lord's glories.

3. Know and avoid illusion (*maya*)

To improve our chanting, it is essential to understand the principle of *maya*. *Maya* refers to "that which is not" or illusion. To grasp this concept, we can use a simple example. According to the scriptures of all traditions, God is the creator of the universe and the most loving father of all living entities. Therefore, we are neither controllers nor creators of this world. However, when a living entity thinks of themselves as "all-powerful" or "all-important," they are under the influence of *maya*, as they are identifying with something that is not real. Similarly, the body is perishable and offers only fleeting pleasures. If we continually try to gratify this temporary body, hoping to find eternal happiness, we are also in *maya*, identifying with a temporary reality. When we are trapped by the workings of this material world and fail to re-establish our loving relationship with God, we are said to be in *maya*.

The energy of *maya* (often referred to in the feminine gender) constantly threatens to divert a yogi from the path of self-realization. Srila Prabhupada once said that *maya* will test a Bhakti yogi thoroughly until the very end of their life. *Maya* tests us to determine whether we truly want to serve Krishna or if we merely want to disturb Him. Many temptations and obstacles arise in the life of a Bhakti yogi. If the devotee survives these tests, their progress to the next level is ensured. If they fail, they remain stuck at that level until they consciously decide to rise above it by rejecting *maya*. At every stage of spiritual progress, *maya* tests the devotee through different challenges.

For a new Bhakti yogi, *maya* may present gross sense pleasures as distractions. By saying "no" to these temptations, the yogi can successfully navigate this phase. However, as the devotee advances spiritually, the tests become subtler and more difficult. Radhanath Swami warns that *maya's* arsenal is vast; for seasoned chanters, she has the subtler weapons of desire for prestige, honor, and respect. As a devotee chants their prescribed number of rounds of the *Hare Krishna* maha mantra daily, they must also check their aspirations. To the extent that we keep our motives pure and cultivate a genuine desire to be the servant of God and all His servants, we remain protected from *maya* and continue to make steady progress on the path of Bhakti-Yoga. Srila Prabhupada and Radhanath Swami's golden formula is to *always remain humble*.

For a sincere practitioner, *maya's* external attacks are relatively easy to handle. The real challenge arises when the attack takes the form of quarrels and dissension among fellow practitioners. Radhanath Swami wisely observes, "*Maya* has no power to stop your progress through external forces. Earthquakes, tornadoes, hurricanes, droughts, floods, and army attacks cannot impede your march forward as much as the seed of discontent and disunity within the society of devotees." His solution is: "We can protect ourselves from the external attacks of *maya* by using intelligence, but to protect ourselves from the subtler, internal attacks, we need humility."

4. Cultivating smallness (humility) and tolerance

The world encourages us to lead a life centered on being a great achiever. Our family and friends often push us to reach impressive heights. However, as practicing spiritualists, we attract God's grace when we cultivate the desire to be small and meek. This is not about losing one's self-respect or sense of worth, but rather about maintaining a constant feeling of dependence on God's mercy. Those who are ill-informed by the materialistic world may criticize this principle of "smallness," but as Jesus Christ said, "It is the meek and humble that shall inherit the kingdom of God."

When a Bhakti yogi adopts the mood of dependence on God, they are protected from distractions on the spiritual path. Srila Prabhupada shares the story of a mouse who was chased by a cat. The mouse sought refuge with a sage, who, using his mystic powers, transformed the mouse into a cat. Grateful, the former mouse continued his life as a cat. However, one day, a dog chased the cat, and once again, the sage transformed the cat into a dog. The danger passed. Later, a tiger attacked the dog, and the sage again intervened, turning the dog into a tiger. The tiger now roamed the jungle fearlessly. One day, feeling hungry, the tiger saw the sage and thought, "Why search elsewhere when this sage could be my lunch?" The sage, understanding the tiger's intentions, sprinkled water on him and recited a spell: "*Punah musika bhava*"– "may you once again become a mouse." In an instant, the tiger was transformed back into a mouse, humbled and deprived of all his previous glory.

Srila Prabhupada narrated this story to highlight how we progress in spiritual life only through the mercy of devotees and Krishna. Initially, we are like infants, small and weak, akin to a mouse in our spiritual journey. However, over time, with sincere effort, we grow and become like tigers, powerful in our spiritual progress and capable of influencing others on their own paths. Yet, if we do not consciously maintain the mood of dependence on God for our service, we risk forgetting the grace of the Lord upon us. We begin to think that we are special and lose sight of the source of our spiritual strength. As we take on senior positions and accumulate possessions, we subtly defy God. At such times, the Lord, through His various energies, humbles us and brings us back to our original, humble state, like a mouse again. This is done through the workings of *maya*, the illusory energy, which lures a Bhakti yogi away from the path by offering many distractions. Therefore, it is crucial for a Krishna yoga practitioner to always remain humble and meek.

Radhanath Swami's reflection on this is both poetic and thought provoking:

> *"The great like to see greatness in others, and the smallness in themselves. The small, on the other hand, see smallness in others and greatness in themselves. That's how you know whether you are small or great."*

Humility, often misunderstood as a weakness, is actually a powerful quality that few truly tap into. Srila Prabhupada explains, "Humility means the freedom from the anxiety of having the satisfaction of being honored by others." In contrast, pride drives us to seek honor from others as a source of happiness. When a proud person is disrespected, his lack of freedom becomes painfully obvious; driven by pride, he loses his composure and reacts with words and actions that often hurt both the other person and himself far more than the situation warrants.

On the other hand, humility brings freedom from the need for external validation and empowers us to act for our own well-being, as well as for the long-term good of everyone. Radhanath Swami offers valuable insight with this statement:

> *"Humility doesn't mean that we let others trample upon us without protesting, but that we don't let others' (mis)behavior determine our decisions and lives. Humility allows us to calmly consider the cause of disrespect and maturely adopt a principled course of action to clarify the situation and rectify the misdemeanor."*

In essence, humility doesn't mean passive submission, but rather, it is the strength to rise above external circumstances, maintain inner peace, and act in a way that is for the ultimate benefit of all.

Cultivating tolerance

Srila Prabhupada once said, "One's greatness is estimated by one's ability to tolerate provoking situations."

How does a *Hare Krishna* chanter cultivate tolerance? The *Śrīmad-Bhāgavatam* gives us a powerful example using the metaphor of forest fires. A forest fire is not intentionally started by anyone; the wind blows, the bamboos rub against each other, and friction causes the fire. Similarly, in the forest of the material world, individual egos clash, often without ill motives or prejudices, resulting in accusations and conflicts. In such moments, we should remember a sacred verse from the *Chaitanya Charitamrita*, where Lord Chaitanya says, "One who thinks himself lower than the grass, who is more tolerant than a tree, and who does not expect personal honor but is always prepared to give all respect to others can very easily always chant the holy name of the Lord" *(Chaitanya Charitamrita, Antya 20.21)*. A tree, despite enduring bitter winters and harsh summers, silently offers its life for the benefit of others without ever retaliating.

Whenever a tendency to judge, criticize, or quarrel arises in our minds, we can try to recall this verse. The scriptures also teach that as *Hare Krishna* chanters, we should thread this verse onto the string of the Holy Name of Krishna and wear it around our necks, just like a talisman. In India, people often wear amulets, precious gems, or astrological stones for protection from evil or disease. However, Lord Chaitanya reminds us that the true protective amulet against quarrels and dissensions is the jewel of humility and tolerance.

The cultivation of noble qualities like tolerance and humility attracts the Lord's grace. A child once asked his father why he should be humble, and the wise father replied, "My child, when you choose the lowly path, there is no place to fall, and the only way is up." We rise because the compassionate Lord notices our desire to be meek and humble. Cultivating this quality is essential for good chanting of *Hare Krishna*.

5. Adding S.A.L.T in our prayer

"The food has no salt," Satish feebly protested. Priya winced and quickly rushed to add salt to his meal.

Satish never thanked his wife for adding salt, yet if she forgot even once, there would be a minor panic at the dinner table. Like Satish, many of us who eat three meals a day take salt for granted. However, salt is arguably the most critical ingredient in any good meal.

Similarly, our spiritual practices can feel lacking or irritable without the right "salt." When we add this essential ingredient, our spiritual diet of prayer, chanting, and hearing becomes nourishing and fulfilling.

SALT stands for *sorry, ask, listen, and thanks.*

S – Sorry

A devotee's prayer session includes a genuine "sorry" for the mistakes made, especially in relationships. The chanting session can be challenging, with the mind often wandering, making it hard to focus on the holy names. At such times, offering a sincere apology to the Lord for being unable to connect helps establish that connection right in that moment.

A – Ask

Just as a child would ask their parents for something they desperately need, a spiritual practitioner prays to Krishna for the gifts that will help them grow closer to God. We urgently need qualities like humility, forgiveness, and tolerance to win Krishna's love. Asking for these blessings during our prayers is a way of emotionally connecting with Him.

L – Listen

Chanting *japa* involves listening to the Holy Names as they vibrate softly on our lips and as we move the beads with our fingers. Listening attentively to the sound of the names is same as listening to Krishna directly. In this age, the Lord incarnates as the Holy Names, so when we listen to our chanting, we are essentially listening to God. He speaks to us when we are present in our prayers.

T – Thanks

At the end of each day, take a moment to reflect on the happy moments and express gratitude for them. Just as a trader sells stocks to earn money, a spiritualist gives thanks to earn spiritual wealth. If, in a prayer session of five to ten minutes, we thank God for the blessings of the past twenty-four hours, we invite happier experiences the following day. Looking back with gratitude allows us to move forward with hope and faith.

In the next two chapters we will explore the power of gratitude.

To stay physically healthy, doctors suggest we eat three times a day and exercise for at least thirty minutes daily. To remain spiritually fit, let us pray three times a day and engage in practical services—our spiritual "exercise"—for at least thirty minutes.

But don't forget the SALT in your prayer diet.

Many sincere spiritual practitioners struggle with a wandering mind. Despite their earnest efforts to serve, pray, and slow down their lives, they often fall victim to the demands of a busy, fast-paced world.

Journaling is a powerful tool that can help slow down the overactive mind. By reflecting on one's thoughts and experiences, journaling allows a practitioner to gain clarity and focus, redirecting mental energy toward spiritual growth.

We will explore the benefits and techniques of journaling in depth in our next chapter.

Part D

Journaling

CHAPTER 4

Diary (Journaling)

> *"While contemplating the objects of the senses, a person develops attachment for them, and from such attachment lust develops, and from lust anger arises. From anger, complete delusion arises, and from delusion bewilderment of memory. When memory is bewildered, intelligence is lost, and when intelligence is lost one falls down again into the material pool."*
>
> —*The Bhagavad Gita* (2.62-63)

Smita was shell-shocked. "He was all right until yesterday. What just happened to him?" Her partner, Ritesh, had impulsively grabbed the chapatti rolling board from the kitchen and hurled it at her with full force. It narrowly missed her. This was just the beginning. The next day, he violently flung her against the wall and kicked her.

They had been together for a year, and she had always seen him as a true gentleman, an epitome of chivalry. When he suggested they move in together, she readily agreed, but she was soon betrayed. The man she thought she knew had turned into someone unrecognizable. A few days later, he begged for forgiveness, promising it would never happen again. For a brief time, he seemed like the kind, noble man she had fallen for. Yet, before long, he repeated his violent outbursts.

The decision to break up was anything but easy, but Smita knew she had to escape the toxic relationship. She eventually found the strength to start a new life.

Another year went by, and one day she met Paresh online. He seemed like the prince charming she had always dreamed of. Paresh found her equally captivating, and they began dating. Smita couldn't believe her luck when he proposed—he was wealthy, handsome, and unfailingly courteous. She felt that, at last, fate had smiled upon her, promising a beautiful life ahead.

However, a few months into their marriage, cracks began to show. One day, without warning, Paresh exploded in anger, hurling abuses at her before slapping her. Smita was stunned. Soon, she uncovered the harsh truth: Paresh was not only cheating on her but also battling severe addiction to drugs.

The betrayal and pain were overwhelming, leaving her heartbroken. After enduring a tumultuous and painful divorce, Smita resolved to rebuild her life. Slowly but steadily, she began to piece together the fragments of her shattered world, determined to reclaim her strength and happiness.

During both tumultuous periods of her life, one thing remained constant: her habit of journaling. Since her early teens, inspired by Anne Frank's *The Diary of a Young Girl*, she had maintained a diary. Anne, a Jewish girl hiding from Nazi persecution during the Holocaust, became a symbol of hope and resilience. Though she didn't realize it at the time, Smita was drawn to Anne's story, fantasizing about escaping her own troubled home and gaining posthumous fame through her diary.

Like any teenager, Smita had her own dreams and aspirations, which evolved over the years. But one thing remained constant: her journal, her faithful companion.

In 2017, after two failed relationships, Smita made a solemn vow: she would never get entangled with another man again. Around this time, she attended my day-long journaling workshop in Birmingham, the vibrant second city of the United Kingdom. Journaling wasn't new to her, but the techniques I shared—which we'll explore in detail in this chapter—were a revelation. They felt like a breath of fresh air, transforming her perspective on the practice.

Smita realized that while she had been diligent in keeping a diary, she had been approaching it in a way that perpetuated her struggles. Her focus had been on answering the wrong questions: "Why is my life bad?", "Why am I suffering so much?", "Why is fate so cruel to me?" This "why" mindset had become the operating system of her journaling, trapping her in a cycle of negativity and self-doubt.

In the workshop, I suggested a shift in focus: to explore "what" questions instead: "What is truly important to me?", "What is the goal of my life?", and "What steps can I take to make my life beautiful?" This simple but powerful shift opened a new chapter in her journaling journey, empowering her to focus on clarity, purpose, and actionable change.

She thanked me after the workshop, expressing gratitude for the shift from a *"why"* to a *"what"* mindset. Her eyes sparkled with newfound hope as she shared her life's challenges. She could now see a glimmer of light amidst the darkness. She also introduced me to her mother, a dignified woman in her late fifties who had weathered many storms. I learned about her harrowing escape from Idi Amin's brutal regime in East Africa during the early 1970s and her subsequent asylum in England.

Although I didn't have much time to engage with her personally, given the numerous participants and events during my month-long stay in the UK, I was deeply impressed by her resilience. Soon, the mother and daughter faded into the background of my life, as I became engrossed in my own world.

Five years later, in 2022, I encountered Smita and her mother again, this time in Coventry. To my surprise, Smita introduced me to Jinal, a charming Gujarati man who had been her husband for the past three years. As soon as I saw her, memories of her story flooded back. What struck me most was how much younger and happier she appeared now—a stark contrast to the Smita I had met years ago. Yet, my skeptical mind couldn't help but wonder: Is this happiness real? Or is it another illusion? Could he, too, be hiding a darker side?

Smita, however, seemed radiant and confident. With a smile, she held both her mother's and Jinal's hands and said, "Our story is living proof of how journaling can transform lives." Her words piqued my curiosity. The three of them warmly insisted I come over for lunch to hear the full story, and I couldn't resist their enthusiasm.

We scheduled a lunch meeting at their home two days later, and I felt a surge of excitement, eager to learn about the next chapter in her remarkable journey.

It was one of the most illuminating conversations I have ever had. Smita revealed that after the workshop, she diligently began keeping an "awareness journal" and a "prayer journal," two types of journaling we will explore in depth in this chapter. At the time, she was single and still healing from the trauma of her painful divorce. She often faced blank pages and a lack of inspiration during her early morning journaling sessions. Yet, she persevered with her daily thirty-minute writing practice.

Over time, something remarkable happened. Layers of her consciousness began to peel away, revealing insights she had never accessed before.

One morning, in an almost magical moment of clarity, she experienced a sudden flash of understanding. In that instant, she grasped why she had been drawn to men like Paresh and Ritesh, and even why Anne Frank's diary had resonated so deeply with her. It was as though she had tapped into a hidden layer of her mind—a deeper truth that had been waiting to be uncovered.

Smita's mother had fled Uganda with her parents during the tumultuous 1970s and later married a Kenyan Gujarati man in London. Together, they had two daughters. Smita's father was an incorrigible alcoholic who often lashed out violently at his wife. Even as a toddler, Smita remembered her mother silently enduring his abuse while still managing to care for the family. Her mother juggled a job, the education of her daughters, and the task of keeping the family stable as her husband's addiction spiraled out of control. Eventually, her father became bedridden, requiring an end-of-life care. Despite everything, Smita's mother shouldered this responsibility with quiet resilience, caring for her husband while continuing to support her daughters.

Witnessing her mother's suffering left a deep imprint on Smita's impressionable mind. She subconsciously internalized the belief that a woman's life was meant to be one of endurance and sacrifice, just like her mother's. Although she outwardly wished for a better life, her subconscious had other plans. Smita unknowingly resigned herself to a path similar to her mother's, attracting men like her father—abusive and unreasonable.

This realization hit her during a particular morning journaling session. As she wrote, the layers of her mind seemed to unravel, and she suddenly understood why she had been drawn to men like Paresh and Ritesh and why Anne Frank's story of hiding from the Nazis had resonated so deeply with her. She realized she, too, sought to hide from her suffering. On the surface, she sought refuge from her travail at home, but deep down, she had accepted her fate as one of inevitable hardship, mirroring her mother's life.

In that moment of clarity, Smita saw how her past had shaped her belief system and how this belief system had unconsciously dictated her choices, leading her to recreate her mother's struggles. Intellectually, she may have encountered such ideas before, but it was through the act of journaling that the full picture of her life's journey came into focus.

This realization was her liberation. She understood not only *what* was wrong but also felt a renewed determination to change her life. The morning pages had broken the chains of her past, giving her the clarity and strength to rewrite her story.

Along with her practices of Krishna consciousness, she diligently maintained a prayer and gratitude journal. As she deepened her spiritual practice, she grew increasingly confident in herself and in the divine plan for her life.

Months later, she met Jinal, and she knew this time was different. She was pleasantly surprised to discover a shift in her perception of men. Through her healing journey, she had come to realize that men could be caring, reasonable, sober, and responsible—qualities Jinal embodied effortlessly. Today, she is a proud mother of two beautiful children, and her family life is filled with joy and harmony.

#1 How Does Journaling Help Emotionally?

Regular journaling allows us to access a deeper, truer version of ourselves. However, our restless mind—if you recall *Chanchal* from Chapter 1—often prevents us from connecting with this inner beauty. When we overthink, the violent fluctuations of neurochemicals in our brain lead us to live a superficial and unfulfilling life.

Daily journaling provides an antidote to this chaos. By transferring worries from our mind onto paper, we create space in our brain for clarity and creativity. Instead of being preoccupied with storing problems, the brain becomes free to solve them. This process is akin to clearing out unnecessary files from a cluttered hard drive. Just as a clean stomach makes us feel physically light and fit, a decluttered mind brings emotional lightness and health. In this space of clarity, we begin to see that the issues our mind magnified were rarely the real problem; there was always something deeper to discover.

Journaling acts as a cleansing mechanism, peeling away the many veils we wear in our social and private lives. The more authentic and unpretentious we become, the easier it is to shed self-delusions about who we are and what we mean to the world. This journey of self-discovery through journaling is transformative, helping us reconnect with our true purpose and essence.

The true story of Manish and Rita mirrors the dynamics of our inner world. Manish represents you, and Rita is like your mind, often driven by emotions and irrational thoughts.

Rita was furious that Manish had been coming home late from the office for the fourth consecutive day. He was tempted to remind her of the agreement they had made—that he would work late to earn extra money for their family's trips to India. "How could she go back on this now?" he thought. But, instead of reacting, he held back. He had learned from relationship seminars that, in moments of emotional explosions, one must first understand the other person before responding. "Let me rephrase what she is saying and reflect back her feelings," Manish thought, and decided to listen with empathy, even though he knew she was wrong in her accusations.

After a few minutes of patient listening, Manish began to uncover the true issue behind Rita's anger. Her complaint wasn't really about his late hours at work—it was about feeling unsupported in the home. She was exhausted from cooking and cleaning alone, and she felt abandoned because he wasn't helping in the kitchen. Manish's first instinct was to defend himself, but he chose again not to react. Instead, he nodded and calmly responded, "You really wish I helped in the kitchen more often."

Still fuming, Rita snapped, "Yes! I have to do it all by myself and you don't care!" Manish's heart burned with frustration, but he remembered the advice his older brother had given him when he first got married: "When one of you is going crazy, the other needs to stay calm. Both can't afford to lose it!"

Despite his internal rage, Manish remained composed. He reminded himself that they had agreed earlier that he would handle the groceries and cleaning, and the kitchen would be her domain. Yet, he refrained from pointing this out. Instead, he continued to listen.

Over time, the real source of Rita's distress slowly revealed itself. Her anger about the kitchen was just a mask for her deeper pain. She was upset that, due to their financial difficulties, they hadn't been able to visit her parents in India for over two years—something that had previously been a regular part of her life. She missed her parents terribly but couldn't express the sadness she felt. Instead, she had focused on her anger at Manish's late hours and his lack of help in the kitchen.

It took Manish's patience, reflection, and empathy to help her understand what was truly bothering her. After nearly half an hour of bickering, Rita sat quietly beside her husband on the sofa, tears in her eyes. They shared a long, silent moment, feeling the depth of their unfulfilled desire. While the pain of their situation remained, the fact that Manish had truly understood her, without judgment, brought a sense of peace and connection to their relationship.

This story is a beautiful reflection of how, often, our emotions—like Rita's—mask deeper pains or unmet needs. Just as Manish patiently listened and empathized with Rita, we too can learn to connect to ourselves. Often, what appears to be frustration or anger on the surface is a signal that there is something deeper we need to address. By reflecting, journaling, and empathizing with ourselves, we can uncover the true source of our emotions and find peace, much like Rita and Manish did.

Our minds, like Rita in the story, often mask deeper concerns with superficial ones. We might find ourselves constantly thinking, "Check your WhatsApp!" or "What's for dinner?" These seemingly trivial thoughts are often distractions from deeper, unresolved issues.

By regular journaling, we can delve beyond the surface-level chatter of the mind, known as *vaikari.* We can move towards *madhyama* speech, where we begin to discern the subtle undercurrents of our thoughts. Ultimately, we can reach *pashyanti* feelings, tapping into the deeper, unspoken emotions that drive our behavior. (Please refer to the previous chapter for details of three levels of sound or prayer).

Through regular journaling, we might discover that our constant thoughts and worries are rooted in more intense issues such as a need for approval, fear of rejection, or a desire for control. Beneath the surface, our minds may be crying out for increased connection and security. We might realize that our true need is to feel loved and accepted, or to overcome our fear of loss.

These emotions are often abstract and elusive, lacking clear words or definitions. They manifest as fragmented thoughts and feelings. The journey of self-reflection allows us to move beyond the noise of daily life and connect with the root causes of our mental and emotional unrest. Just as Manish's patience helped Rita reveal her true pain, regular, patient journaling can help us uncover our own deepest emotions and find lasting peace.

My friend Anand Vrindavan Dasa encourages his students to chant *Hare Krishna* early in the morning, before sunrise. But that's just the *vaikari* speech. The *madhyama*, or unseen voice, conveys something deeper: "You'll be in big trouble if you don't chant in the early morning, because the mind is nasty. It will degrade you to lower levels of consciousness." This is the underlying message he intends to communicate. Yet, even subtler than that is Anand Vrindavan's true appeal: compassion and love. If it could be expressed in words, it would sound something like, "Krishna loves you, and you can access His love during the quiet hours of the morning. You can feel His love if you chant attentively, and the early morning is the best time to tap into the power of attention."

But not all of this manifests in speech. Externally, his students only hear his urgent plea, "Please chant early in the morning." However, behind these words is a deep concern for their spiritual well-being, and beneath that concern lies his energy of compassion and love.

In much the same way, the mind demands that we watch a movie, sleep, or eat a chocolate. But deeper within is *Chanchal's* pain of feeling unloved or its insecurity about old age. What appears to be an issue on the surface is merely a decoy. There is far more to the drama than what shows up on the screen of the mind.

Journaling, as a practice, helps us hear the real voice of the mind. It is like Manish and Rita sharing silence—it allows us to live comfortably in our own skin. We become aware of what ails the mind, and while we aspire to improve, we are not in a rush to change God's plan for us. We live in acceptance and surrender to the Lord's will. Just as Rita felt grateful that her husband didn't judge her, our mind too begins to cooperate, and our relationship with *Chanchal* improves as we vomit out the clutter we have been storing in our brains, onto paper. It is uncomfortable to throw up, but there is relief afterward.

Journaling can be intense at times, but it is also comforting and cathartic. Plus, there are many scientific benefits that Google and YouTube can reveal. However, in this book, I'll share what I personally do, and this is the kind of advice you won't find on the internet.

#2 Seven Types of Journaling

We will now explore a few common journaling techniques that can help transform our overthinking patterns into a more productive lifestyle. Each of these practices is powerful and can contribute to inner peace.

It is important to note that there is no one-size-fits-all approach to journaling. While some methods may be beneficial, others can lead to unhealthy rumination. For example, as discussed in Smita's case, solely focusing on *"why"* questions can lead to self-doubt and negative thinking. Rather than discovering the truth, we may start inventing answers; instead of developing insights, we may create self-limiting beliefs. This is because the mind is crafty and we cannot easily uncover the truer version of ourselves simply through thought. We can think endlessly for years and still not find clarity. Overthinking is a prime example of how our thinking alone can't solve problems unless we do it the right way.

While spontaneity is valuable in journaling, it is also essential to have a structured approach to ensure consistency.

The techniques I share provide a foundation for your journaling practice, allowing you to eventually develop your unique style of self-expression.

Don't get too caught up in finding the "perfect" way to journal. The most important thing is to start. Consider the following journaling practices as a menu of options, allowing you to choose and combine them as you see fit.

1. Self-awareness journal

You simply write about your various thoughts, in third person, and without judgment.

It is like switching on a video camera inside of you. Right now, if there were a video camera outside of you, what would it note about you? As for me, a camera would objectively record me sitting in an airport waiting area, writing a book. It would capture the bustling crowd of travelers and the fact that I have been writing uninterrupted for the past two hours. The camera wouldn't judge whether my writing is good or bad, or whether the airport is hot or cold. It wouldn't care if I'm hungry or tired. It would simply record what it sees. A human observer, however, would likely form opinions and judgments about my actions.

Now, let us turn the camera inward. Can you observe your thoughts without judgment? What is your mind saying right now?

My awareness journal entry for last Monday was as follows:

It is 5 a.m., and I can hear Chanchal urging me to take a quick shower and rush to the temple for Mangal Arati. It is concerned that others might object to my missing the morning community program. Then, it adds, "Rajesh is haughty and needs to be taught a lesson." But now, Chanchal says, "It's okay if you miss it; you're spending quality time writing in your journal." Now it insists, "But you should finish the journal entry quickly," only to immediately follow with, "But, then again, take your time."

It is silent now; as if it is at peace and has nothing to say. I'm not thinking about anything at the moment.

I take a few deep breaths and notice Chanchal's voice again. It suggests I check my emails and reply to Pawan's concern. It says I need to inform Pawan and even Malati about my change in travel plans. It mentions that Kolkata will be hot this time of year, so I shouldn't bother bringing a sweater. It recalls my last visit to Kolkata, where I stayed in a fancy hotel and traveled for eight hours to reach Mayapur. It is upset that I missed an opportunity to please Chaitanya Dasa, who had asked me to conduct a seminar for the leaders. And now, Chanchal is reminding me it is time to go to the toilet and shower.

Once again, it falls silent.

The awareness journal is a simple, yet incredibly effective tool to help you separate yourself from your mind.

Remember, your mind is constantly chattering on your left side (as discussed in Chapter 1), and you want to turn to your right and listen to Krishna's voice. Chanchal, the voice of your mind, is loud and insistent, always demanding attention. It is never at peace; it always has something to say and expects you to listen—like an obedient servant. It has you completely under its grip. You may have tried to break free from its hold by resisting, and that may have worked for a while, but as you get older, it smirks. It knows you'll eventually give in. You'll do anything to quieten it, even if it means surrendering to its demands.

But deep within, there is a desire to turn toward your higher self, to hear Krishna's voice, and to follow His divine guidance. For years, your spirit was strong enough to resist, but now both your body and mind are growing weaker. You can't keep fighting the mind.

It is time to change your approach. Shift from struggle—with the mind—to surrender—to Krishna. And surrender begins with awareness and acceptance of your situation.

When you simply write down what the mind is proposing, without judging yourself, you practice both awareness and acceptance. It is like stopping the argument with your spouse and instead, trying to understand what she's saying. Stephen Covey popularized this method in his book *The Seven Habits of Highly Effective People*, where he says, "First seek to understand, then, to be understood." This principle applies to your inner spouse, Chanchal, as well. When you spend a few minutes writing down whatever the mind is suggesting, you'll notice that eventually, the mind goes quiet. It has nothing more to say. It is peaceful. That's when you can hear your Lord's voice. When the mind is loud, you are disconnected from Krishna.

Sometimes during temple *kirtans*, the sound of drums and cymbals, amplified by the loudspeakers, can make it impossible to hear a devotee's request. We step outside the hall to listen to what they are saying. Similarly, when the mind's noise is overwhelming, you can't hear your real self—or God—trying to communicate. You need to retreat to a quieter space, like the room of your journal, with paper and pen. There, you first write down what the mind is saying. When it quietens, you can turn to Krishna and hear His voice more clearly (more on this in the next section on the 'prayer' journal).

You'll be amazed and amused as you attempt to write the mind's proposals. Sometimes, you'll begin writing a sentence that the mind suggests, only for it to suddenly jump to another topic, leaving you wondering what you intended to write. The sentence might look like this: *"Chanchal now says I shouldn't have eaten so much last night. What time is the morning class? Who left the lights on outside the bathroom? Where are the bills to be signed?"* Other times, you'll realize the mind has jumped through fifty different topics in just ten seconds. It is like watching a movie where the protagonist, Mr. Mind, is running at 4x speed, and you're trying to keep up with what he's doing or saying. Up until now, you have been following the commands of this despot, but suddenly you realize you're not obliged to obey him. You also see that he's not really your boss. It is okay to simply note what he says. And then, there is no struggle. He's not a cruel dictator after all. He just needs acceptance in your inner world. You need to allow him to be who he is.

In the first chapter, we explored the five *koshas*, or sheaths, that cover the real self. One of them is the *manomaya kosha*, the sheath of the mind. When we're disturbed, we often say, "I am sad" or "I am angry." But the more we practice the awareness journal, the more we can separate ourselves from the drama of the mind. We may eventually find ourselves spontaneously saying, "My mind is sad" or "My mind is angry." Notice the huge difference between these two phrases—"I am miserable" and "My mind is gloomy." The second statement clarifies that *you* are fine, while it is the mind that is irritable or melancholy.

Awareness, therefore, is key to developing stronger emotional intelligence. Recognizing and acknowledging our mental state is the first step. From there, we can discern, with our higher awareness, which thoughts and emotions to take seriously and which to release. In other words, overthinking gives way to effective thinking and conscious living. This is how we grow emotionally and evolve spiritually.

2. Prayer journal

A prayer journal is a space where you express your heartfelt aspirations to God. You bring your love, wishes, fears, and hopes before Krishna, all conveyed through writing. The power of a prayer journal lies in the energy of your emotions, and the next chapter will delve deeper into the role emotions play in this practice.

Many sincere spiritual practitioners find prayer to be a challenging art. It may feel as though God is far away, while the mind—our closest companion—demands all of our attention and service. However, an advanced Bhakti yogi has the opposite realization. They come to understand that Krishna, not the mind, is our closest companion. The mind is a distant and inconsequential part of our lives. A pure devotee of Krishna experiences a truth far beyond the petty bickering of the mind. Bhakti-Yoga is fundamentally a journey—from seeing the mind as our closest companion to discovering Krishna as the supersoul (*parmatma*), our eternal and truest friend, residing within our hearts. As a result, we begin to live a life that transcends the proposals and anxieties of the mind. The mind no longer matters when our life is centered on regular prayers and a deep connection with Krishna.

You may admit that you haven't reached this stage yet, so what's your hope? Try adding the technique of combining an awareness journal with your prayer journal. Let me explain how.

When you write a prayer to God and feel that the prayer doesn't truly reflect your heart, pause. Stop writing the prayer, switch to your awareness journal, and keep writing down what the mind is saying until it quietens. Once Chanchal—the voice of the mind—is silent, return to your prayer journal and continue the prayer. You'll notice a remarkable difference between the two versions—the one you first wrote and the one you wrote after the awareness journal.

A glimpse into my prayer journal:

Krishna, I love you, I really wish to serve you. I want to feel your love in my heart.

Chanchal is angry at me for travelling so far. It is happy we came here because there are so many nice people in this city. It says Pajaka temple is crowded and the smoke billowing out of yajna is purifying. Those dhotis and sarees are expensive with rich embroidery. It is quite hot the mind says. Go to washroom now. No, you can wait. Chanchal says you haven't visited Rajapur as yet and it is Navin who is yelling outside. It is now blank and I guess this is my chance.

Krishna, I love you, I really wish to serve you. I want to feel your love in...

Chanchal is now in Remuna and wondering who is singing outside the room. The hot water is not available in this room and the AC makes a lot of sound.

Krishna, I want to please your wonderful devotees. Let me never judge them or offend them...

The first, third, and the fifth paragraph is prayer journal and the second and fourth is awareness journal.

Interspersing our prayers with an awareness journal allows us to return to Krishna with more feeling and depth. The prayer then truly carries our individual voice, making it far more fulfilling when it is you calling out to Krishna, and the mind's noise fades into the background.

In the beginning, when I started writing the first paragraph, the mind's chatter was overwhelming. It was loud, with many things to say, and I felt disconnected both from Krishna and from my own mind. As a result, my prayers lacked the emotional depth needed for a true spiritual connection. So, I shifted my focus to improving my awareness and acceptance of my mental state—recognizing what emotions I was genuinely experiencing. This led to the second paragraph. When the mind felt heard and understood, it calmed down and quieted. This allowed me to then connect with Krishna in the third paragraph.

Switching between these practices helps you move from being tightly bound by the mind's clutches to resting in Krishna's loving arms. The mind no longer occupies the center stage of your life. Instead, a relationship with God begins to emerge, one that is refreshing and full of immense spiritual possibilities.

3. Cringe conversion journal

Do you carry feelings of embarrassment, hurt, or pain in your heart? Have you said or done things in life that you wish you hadn't? Does the mere thought of those incidents make you cringe? Do past events haunt you or threaten your peace? Do you fear that your unpleasant experiences will undermine your future? If so, try the *cringe conversion journal.*

There are three key steps to this practice:

Step – 1

First, write about the incident—when and what happened. Keep the writing objective, focusing on the facts without getting caught up in the emotions connected to the event. You can mention the emotions, but don't write about them emotionally. For example, if I recall an incident from my past, such as blanking out during an inter-school elocution competition, where I was embarrassed in front of my schoolmates, I can now describe the event and the emotions I experienced without getting caught in the intensity of those feelings.

If the incident was traumatic, it may be difficult to separate the emotions from the event. In such cases, it is helpful to consult a professional for support. At the same time, you can complement this with journaling. If you can't yet separate yourself from the emotions tied to the event, that's okay. Just write whatever you feel—release the pent-up emotions surrounding the incident. The important thing is to get it on paper.

Step – 2

Read it and reread it. Take time to reflect on what happened. Slowly, try to detach from the personal involvement and imagine that this event happened to your best friend, Raj or Anita, rather than you. Picture them writing the same journal entry. Now, read it again as if it were a journal entry written by Raj or Anita.

Step – 3

This is a common human tendency: we are often better at giving advice than taking it ourselves. By imagining that your friend, Raj or Anita, is going through the same experience, you can gain a fresh perspective. Write a letter to your friend, offering words of comfort and support.

By the end of the third step, you will have solutions, empathy, support, and reassurances from a loving friend. When you read what you have written, you may be surprised by the many solutions your mind can offer. When it was your problem, you were mentally stuck. But when it is your friend's suffering, your mind generates plenty of ideas to help.

By empathizing with your friend, you can unlock your own wisdom and compassion.

A friend of mine lost his teenage son in a freak accident on the road outside their house. Understandably, both parents were devastated. Even three years later, the mother couldn't forgive herself for what she felt was her fault—letting her son cross the street while she was talking to him from the other side. She believed that if she had waited for him to cross and then spoken to him, he might have been more cautious of the speeding car that struck him, crushing his skull. The guilt and pain from the loss took a heavy toll on her health. She practically stopped eating, and even when her parents forced her to eat, she could never bring herself to consume food that her son had liked.

Her husband, my close friend, was at a loss as to how to help her. I suggested they consult a professional emotional healer, and in the meantime, I shared the three steps outlined above. She began writing a letter to "her friend" every day and, without realizing it, practiced self-compassion in the process.

This is one of her journal entries—notice the amazing counselling or advice she got, ironically from herself:

"You were an amazing mother. You fed him his favorite panipuris and sandwiches whenever he insisted. He loved you so much that, even at fifteen, when most boys are rebellious and independent, he'd hold you tight as he slept at night. You filled his heart with so much love for you that he never kept any secrets from you. Isn't this the highest example of motherhood? The Śrīmad-Bhāgavatam says a mother's duty is to facilitate her son's journey to God. The fact that, during the last two days, as he grappled with life and death, he constantly chanted the Holy Names, even in a semi-conscious state, proves he had perfected his life—thanks to his loving parents.

Besides, when you die, you'll have to give up everything that you hold dear. You got a sample of death—seeing what it means to lose what's most precious to you. And we are supposed to be grateful at that moment. Most people can't practice gratitude when God bestows so many gifts upon them; how will they express thanks when, at death, it is all going to be taken away? You can thank God for the beautiful gift you had for fifteen years of your life, and the Lord has taken it away from you now. He had to take it sooner or later.

Do you realize this pain will help you assist so many suffering people in this world? Remember, a wounded healer is the best healer. You have suffered so intensely, and now, when you counsel others in pain, you will illuminate their lives with hope and strength. Many mothers lose their sons in war, but they find solace in the fact that their sons martyred their lives for the country. You, too, can take solace in the fact that your son is a martyr in the Lord's army, which is protecting humanity from heartache and grief. You had to lose your son so that you could now help those anguished by the reactions of material energy..."

4. Wisdom journal

> *"Realization means you should write, every one of you, what is your realization... You write your realization, what you have realized about Krishna. That is required. It is not passive. Always you should be active. Whenever you find time, you write. Never mind, two lines, four lines, but you write your realization... You are hearing, but you have to write also. Then write means smaranam, remembering what you have heard...."*
>
> —Srila Prabhupada lecture (August 4, 1972, Los Angeles)

There are countless amazing TED Talks and podcasts available online. You could spend an entire day watching them and have many "aha" moments. However, simply consuming this data won't help much unless you internalize what you learn.

One of the simplest and most effective ways to internalize knowledge is by writing it down. And the best part? It costs nothing.

Many people take notes during our morning classes at the temple, where the speaker presents a systematic discussion on a particular verse from the sacred wisdom text *Śrīmad Bhāgavatam*. But that's not the type of writing I'm referring to here. When we jot down what the speaker says, it is essentially a process of transferring knowledge from their mind to our notebook. Later, by reviewing these notes, we transfer the same information from the notebook to our mind. This is a *head-to-head* transfer—an intellectual exchange.

But there is another way to write—one that facilitates a *heart-to-heart* transmission.

Here is how it works: First, listen to the class or read the scriptures as attentively as possible. Even if your mind wanders, gently bring your focus back. As you listen or read, engage not just your ears or eyes, but also your heart. Try to sense the mood of the speaker or the essence of the passage. What feelings, insights, or realizations does it evoke in you?

Later, in a quiet space, open your notebook and start writing what you understood from the class or reading. Write anything and everything you remember, liked, or learned—but in your *own words*. Feel free to connect it to other things you have heard, read, or experienced. There are no strict rules here. What matters is that when you write it down, it becomes *yours*.

When we write in this way, it is no longer just the speaker's knowledge—it transforms into our realization. For instance, if you attend a morning class on the *Śrīmad Bhāgavatam* and later write a short essay about it, those insights become a part of you.

Despite the abundance of wisdom available today, why don't we see more lives transformed by it? The answer lies in our focus: we emphasize *information* over *transformation*.

My mentor in the monastery introduced me to a simple yet powerful approach to create transformational knowledge. After I attended a class or read a book, he wouldn't ask, "What did you hear or read?" Instead, he'd ask, "What did you learn?" That distinction is crucial. Hearing or reading is just the first step; the second, more significant step is learning. After I shared what I'd learned, he'd then ask, "How can you apply this in your life?"

From these conversations, I came to understand the three essential steps to internalizing wisdom: *hearing (or reading), learning,* and *applying.*

In Sanskrit, these steps are beautifully captured as *śravaṇam* (hearing), *mananam* (reflection), and *nididhyāsanam* (application).

Hearing or reading is the starting point, where knowledge enters through the ears (or eyes). But without reflection—*mananam*—it may simply exit from the other ear. When we reflect and introspect, the knowledge finds a deeper place within us. It begins to guide, direct, and protect us, becoming our companion on the journey of life. Writing plays a vital role in this process, as it helps us reflect and internalize better.

Transformation begins when we actively engage with what we learn—by thinking deeply, writing with intention, and applying it in our daily lives.

Many religious groups have followers who hear teachings but don't reflect on them, reducing the practice to a mere ritual. Others may introspect deeply but neglect to draw wisdom from external sources or traditional teachings. Such reflection can become a form of sophisticated speculation, disconnected from a higher reality.

We need a balance of both—wisdom from a higher source and our own reflections. *Nidhidhyāsanam,* the practice of applying knowledge, takes this a step further. Even a small amount of applied knowledge is more valuable than vast amounts of stored knowledge. By seeking to apply what we learn, we move knowledge from the ear to the head, and ultimately, to the heart.

Bhakti-Yoga teachers introduce a fourth step in the wisdom journey: *vandanam*, or prayer. After hearing, learning, and applying, we offer prayers to the Divine, seeking blessings to use our knowledge in the service of God and humanity. This practice keeps us humble and fosters a student-like attitude of continuous learning and growth.

Additionally, the culture of prayer cultivates curiosity as we observe the world around us.

Curiosity vs. Cynicism

One of my teachers, His Holiness Sacinandana Swami, has been a practicing spiritualist for over five decades. Despite having many disciples and followers and being widely respected for his classes and *kirtans*, he regularly attends the classes of younger Bhakti-Yoga practitioners—both men and women, many of whom weren't even born when he began his journey in Krishna consciousness.

In one of his teachings, he explained his approach: he prefers to be like a mango that is "green and growing" rather than a fruit that is "ripe and rotting." When we remain "green," we are curious and open to learning. In contrast, when we imagine that we already know everything there is to understand, we delude ourselves into thinking we are fully "ripened." This mindset marks the beginning of spiritual stagnation, similar to a fruit starting to rot.

Maintaining a regular practice of journaling about wisdom or scriptures helps us stay curious and engaged as students on the path of Bhakti-Yoga. It protects us from becoming fanatical or dogmatic, fostering instead a thoughtful and reflective approach to what we hear and learn. More importantly, it keeps the child within us alive—the child who sees the world as a place of endless possibilities.

Dr. A.P.J. Abdul Kalam, former President of India, affectionately known as the "Missile Man of India," expressed this idea beautifully in his book *Ignited Minds*. Having traveled extensively and inspired thousands of children, he often emphasized the importance of maintaining a seeker's mindset. When asked who the world's first scientist was, Dr. Kalam answered to thunderous applause: "A child is the world's first scientist." He explained that children live in a mindset of possibility, constantly exploring and searching for answers. Unfortunately, as many of us grow older and face life's struggles, our curiosity often gives way to cynicism. The child within us is silenced, and life becomes less a refreshing journey of discovery and more a tiresome routine.

Journaling offers a way to rekindle that childlike curiosity.

In another program, Dr. Kalam was once stumped by a child's question. Normally quick to respond, he found himself pondering when the child asked, "Why can't we transfer the excess water from the Brahmaputra River, which floods Assam, to Tamil Nadu and Rajasthan, where there is water scarcity?" For the child, the solution seemed straightforward—a world of possibilities. However, Dr. Kalam knew the complexities of governance, where water is a state issue, and transferring it involves central authority and logistical challenges. Yet, the child's question reminded him of the simplicity and possibility mindset that fuels innovation and change.

The deep mysteries of life are revealed when we nurture a childlike curiosity and a genuine eagerness to learn and explore.

This was the transformative journey of Prince Siddhartha, who became Gautama Buddha. Despite his parents' efforts to shield him from all hardships, one day, while venturing into the city with his charioteer, he encountered the realities of birth, old age, disease, and death. These sights stirred something within him—a burning desire to understand the *why* behind these phenomena. "Why do they exist?", "What is their purpose?". Driven by these questions, he left his home and royal comforts in search of the ultimate truth.

The *Bhagavad Gita* (13.8-12) emphasizes that true knowledge begins with seeking to understand the mysteries of birth, death, old age, and disease. This quest lies at the heart of genuine wisdom.

You might protest, "But I have so many practical problems to solve! I need answers to the *how* questions, not the *why* questions."

When to ask How *and* Why?

As discussed earlier in this book, we navigate two dimensions of reality: the *physical reality*, which involves our daily worries, finances, and responsibilities, and the *metaphysical reality*, which invites us to explore deeper existential questions. The physical reality addresses concerns like earning a living, managing relationships, or completing tasks, while the metaphysical reality compels us to reflect on larger issues: *Who are we in relation to the cosmos? Why is life the way it is? What happens after death?*

When dealing with the physical realm, we often ask *how*: *"How can I solve this problem?", "How can I meet my goals?"* But when exploring the metaphysical plane, we need to shift our focus to *why*: *"Why am I here?", "Why does this matter?"*

Journaling is a powerful tool that can help us navigate both realities. For instance, if you have lost your job, journaling can assist in brainstorming actionable steps for securing new employment. It helps you address practical concerns like *how* to manage daily expenses or meet project deadlines. On the other hand, if you find yourself questioning your place in the universe or the purpose of your existence, journaling allows you to delve into the *why* of life's mysteries.

During our spiritual retreats, when devotees ask questions like, *"How can I improve my meditation practice?"* or *"How can I become more sincere in developing love for God?"*, I often respond by asking them *why*: *"Why do you want to improve your meditation?", "Why do you desire sincerity in your spiritual journey?"* Asking *why* helps uncover the deeper motivations and aspirations driving these goals.

5. How did God (Krishna) show up today?

A couple of years ago, a dear friend, Venkat Bhatt, introduced me to a rewarding type of journaling. Since then, not only has each day felt more meaningful, but I have also started connecting the dots to many mysteries in life.

The practice is simple yet transformative: each night, before retiring, answer one question in your journal: *"How did God show up today?"*

At first, this wasn't easy. For the first few days, my mind went blank, and my journal entries remained empty. But as I persisted, I realized that to answer this question, I needed to stay more attentive to the events of my day. Perhaps God was speaking to me through someone's story, example, or words. I began listening more deeply, hearing unspoken messages in conversations. My eyes started noticing small miracles in ordinary events, and my mind and intelligence worked to process situations beyond their surface appearance. I was beginning to peel back the superficial layers of daily life.

At times, I felt as though I was forcing connections, seeing God's hand in what seemed to be mundane occurrences. It felt contrived, but I continued with the practice, offering a silent prayer to Krishna: *Please help me see Your presence in every aspect of my life.*

Then, one day, something extraordinary happened. I witnessed an event that a few others also saw, yet they missed its divine significance. For me, it was unmistakably a moment where God's presence shone through.

A giant monkey sauntered down the steps from the terrace and appeared outside our rooms on the third floor of the monastery. It was 6 a.m., a time when we are usually at the temple, immersed in our morning prayers. But that day, the ashram was unusually bustling with monks tending to personal chores. When I saw the monkey, panic surged through me. I grabbed my chappals and instinctively raised them, ready to shoo away the intruder. How dare this creature invade our private space? Some rooms were open—what if he caused chaos? The pantry was stocked with fruits, practically an open invitation for mischief. I was determined to stop this audacious trespasser. Yet, the monkey was unimpressed. With a casual wave of his hand, he dismissed my threat and strode confidently into the premises. I followed him nervously, unsure of what he might do. He paused briefly before turning towards the open room of our temple president, Radha Gopinath Das, who sat peacefully sipping his morning medicine.

For a moment, the monkey and Radha Gopinath locked eyes. The monkey raised his hand in what looked like a thumbs-up gesture, then, to my surprise, turned around and headed back. As he passed me, still holding my chappals aloft, he tapped my calves, as if to say, "*Calm down, mortal,*" and climbed back up to the terrace, disappearing into the morning sky.

Most monks resumed their daily activities, brushing off the incident as an unusual but harmless disruption. But I stood there, stunned, trying to process what I had just witnessed. Suddenly, it hit me: this wasn't just any monkey—it was Lord Hanuman himself! Excitedly, I exclaimed to everyone around me that Hanuman had visited to acknowledge and honor Radha Gopinath Das.

The night before, Radha Gopinath had delivered a powerful discourse on the *Ramayana* in honor of *Rama Navami*, Lord Rama's appearance day. He had eloquently recounted Hanuman's heroic exploits, including his legendary burning of Lanka with his blazing tail. Could it be that Hanuman had come to express his gratitude for this glorification?

I ran to Radha Gopinath and declared, "Lord Hanuman just came to thank you for last night's brilliant *Ramayana* class!" Ever humble, he dismissed my interpretation with a laugh, attributing the incident as an ordinary monkey's visit from the nearby Governor's bungalow. But I wasn't convinced.

I presented my case: How many times have you seen a monkey in our temple premises in the 36 years you have lived here? "Never," he admitted. Why did the monkey come mere hours after your *Ramayana* class? Why did he stop specifically at your room and nowhere else? How did he get past the net-sealed terrace, a space no animal or bird has accessed before? By now, a crowd of monks had gathered, listening intently as I rattled off point after point. While most monks glowed with excitement, Radha Gopinath remained stoic, his humility preventing him from accepting my theory.

Still, I argued: *Ramayana* tradition states that wherever Lord Rama's glories are sung, Hanuman is present, even if unseen. Radha Gopinath's purity and sincerity, I reasoned, must have drawn Hanuman's blessing. Everyone nodded in agreement, and one monk commended my logic, marveling that none of them had thought of this connection before.

Later, I realized why this incident stood out so vividly to me: my daily journaling practice of asking, *"How did God show up today?"* had trained my mind to perceive the divine in ordinary events. Even if this was just a "freak incident," my spiritualized consciousness allowed me to see it as extraordinary.

From that day, I approached the Hanuman deity in our temple with a renewed sense of respect and awe. My reading and appreciation of the *Ramayana* deepened, and my relationship with Radha Gopinath Das became better. During temple management meetings, when disagreements arose, I would remind myself, "He is very dear to the Lord—handle this with care." This shift in perception enriched my spiritual life and improved my interactions with others.

Eventually, I shared the story with our guru, Radhanath Swami, eager to hear his perspective. He listened attentively, smiling as I recounted every detail. When I asked if we could conclude that it was indeed Hanuman who had visited, he grinned mischievously and said, "Well, you could light fire to his tail—that would confirm it!"

Seeing God in small things

While dramatic stories like encountering Hanuman are captivating, journaling's power lies equally in helping us recognize divinity in the mundane rhythm of daily life. The extraordinary is thrilling, but the ordinary often holds spiritual insights—if we pause to notice.

Take this simple incident, for instance: yesterday, a woman approached me outside the temple and insisted she had seen my mother waiting for me nearby. I thanked her for the information but clarified that my mother was in Bengaluru, and I had just spoken to her a few hours earlier. Realizing she had likely mistaken someone else for my mom, she apologized, and we parted ways. Seemingly an uneventful interaction, right?

Yet, as I reflected, I saw God's hand in it. Just moments earlier, I had concluded my morning prayers but had forgotten to include any blessings for my mother. The woman's comment suddenly reminded me of this oversight. Feeling a tug in my heart, I returned to the altar and prayed earnestly for my mom, my brothers, and their families. It was as though God had shown up through this woman to nudge me gently—*Don't forget to pray for your mother.* At the time, it felt ordinary, almost insignificant. But as I wrote this chapter, the memory resurfaced, and I saw the divine orchestration in that moment.

Journaling allows us to *pause* our lives, to step out of the frantic rush of daily living. It is like slowing down a speeding car. At 100 km/hr, the trees, birds, and buildings outside the window blur into a single indistinct smear. But when we ease off the accelerator, the details come into focus—we can see the birds perched on the branches, the textures of the leaves, and the play of sunlight on the landscape.

In the same way, our busy lives often blind us to the subtle details of our inner world and God's hand at work. We race forward, driven by the urgency of survival, rarely stopping to reflect. Journaling helps us slow down, giving us a chance to notice beauty, harmony, and rhythm in our lives. More importantly, it helps us align with what God wants from us.

Another incident comes to mind: I was traveling on a train, chanting on my prayer beads. Afterward, I dozed off, leaving my bead bag hooked by the window. When my station arrived, I woke with a start and hurried toward the door to disembark. Suddenly, just as I was about to step off the train, I remembered my bead bag. I dashed back, retrieved it from its precarious perch, and exited the train—barely ten seconds later.

At first, I saw this as a simple case of sudden remembrance, nothing particularly spiritual. But that night, as I sat with my journal, the incident revealed itself differently. It struck me that Krishna might have been the one reminding me. I imagined Him saying, *"You fool, you forgot your bead bag—go and get it!"* If a friend traveling with me had reminded me, I would have thanked him. Similarly, in that moment of journaling, I felt like Krishna had been my companion on that train, kindly helping me avoid losing something so important.

The *Bhagavad Gita* (15.15) states, *"I am seated in everyone's heart, and from Me come remembrance, knowledge, and forgetfulness."* Journaling gave me the clarity to see God's hand in this small event. It wasn't just me remembering—it was Krishna, seated in my heart, prompting me with His gentle guidance.

God is constantly guiding us, arranging situations, and allowing us to act freely. Journaling helps us tune into His voice, which often goes unnoticed amidst life's noise. It slows us down, allowing us to see how He moves through even the smallest details of our lives.

This practice is closely linked to gratitude journaling—the most transformative form of journaling I have experienced. Through it, I have learned not just to *ask* for blessings but to *acknowledge* the countless ways God already blesses me each day.

6. Gratitude journal

A friend of mine, a resident of the ashram, expressed a heartfelt desire to serve his aging father during his final days. Unfortunately, fate had other plans. Even as he was preparing to return home and care for his parents, his father unexpectedly passed away from a cardiac arrest. Devastated and disoriented, he rushed home.

Over the next thirteen days, a steady stream of relatives and friends arrived to offer condolences. Despite his grief, my friend maintained his daily gratitude journaling practice, a habit he had cultivated for over a decade. After the final rites and rituals, he returned to the monastery to resume his spiritual journey.

He shared a realization: *"I was unhappy the whole time I was at home. I cried so often, remembering my father and reflecting on all the ways I could have served him and made him happy. Yet, amidst the sorrow, I felt a strange but powerful sense of peace within. Each day, I wrote my gratitude journal as usual, dedicating time to write about my father. I can't say I was happy—after all, who could be after losing their father? But I felt deeply connected to him, prayerful, and thankful for his presence in my life. It was a beautiful experience—a blend of pain and gratitude."*

Life is undeniably harsh, and it doesn't take long to realize how much suffering exists in the material world. Yet gratitude has the power to anchor us, offering an inexplicable sense of peace even amidst pain. This is the unique gift of gratitude journaling—it enables us to find beauty and meaning in life's most challenging moments.

This sentiment is echoed by a journaling workshop participant, 35-year-old Kalyan, whose letter I share below:

"My sister lived in Norway with her three young children and her husband, a successful lawyer. One day, she was devastated to discover that he had been cheating on her for years. She found out he had a paramour in Sweden with whom he lived for extended periods. Being a lawyer, he had expertly hidden his tracks, and she remained unaware until, by sheer chance, she discovered that he had invested heavily in properties across Scandinavia—under his mistress's name.

Heartbroken, she confronted him, but he coldly walked out on her and went to live with his lover. My sister was left stranded with three small children. Panicked, she called me. As a middle-class Indian without the financial means or a visa to travel to Europe, I felt utterly helpless.

Desperate, I reached out to a devotee friend, who, in turn, contacted his friend in Denmark. This couple, driven by compassion, traveled over 600 kilometers to provide her the emotional support she so desperately needed. They also connected her to a devotee community near her town. After weeks of anxiety and uncertainty, she found herself surrounded by a much-needed support system.

Slowly but surely, my sister began piecing her life back together with the help of these well-wishers.

This morning, as I wrote in my journal, I felt a complex blend of emotions—anger and resentment toward my brother-in-law for his betrayal, but also an overwhelming sense of gratitude and love for the people who rallied around my sister. I was thankful for their kindness, which made me realize that she wasn't alone, even in a foreign land far from home. It was as though she had many brothers and sisters there, stepping in to care for her when she needed it most.

My journal entry was filled with reflections on the fortune of being connected to such a caring community. Despite the pain of the situation, I experienced this contradiction—anger at her husband's treachery, yet gratitude and love for the devotees who helped my sister rebuild her life."

Both the above stories illustrate how journaling can help us navigate complex emotions, allowing us to find gratitude and strength even in the midst of adversity.

Gratitude vs. Happiness

Are happy people grateful? Not necessarily. But are grateful people happy? Absolutely. That's because they access a higher dimension of happiness.

Bhakti-Yoga practices help us tune into the divine voice within. This voice isn't always a gentle whisper of love. It can also be a stern admonishment, pointing out our mistakes and false pride. The more sincere and attentive we are in our Bhakti practices, the more clearly Krishna helps us see our inadequacies. This can be a simultaneously painful and blissful experience.

I'd like to share a personal experience that illuminated this phenomenon for me.

While writing in my prayer-awareness journal one day, I noticed a surge of anger towards a devotee with whom I'd had a falling out years ago. Despite my efforts to reconcile, he remained deeply hurt and blamed me for certain decisions. The accusations became so intense that I had to cut off all communication. At one point, the abuse was so severe that it shook my self-confidence. Anger would flare up whenever I thought of him. Over time, I believed I had forgiven him and moved on, but that day, my mind unleashed a torrent of expletives. I wanted to lash out, to physically harm him. As I returned to my awareness practice, I couldn't help but smile at my mind's ability to dredge up old wounds. In the following days, the anger resurfaced during chanting and journaling. I wondered why this person kept invading my thoughts, seemingly unprovoked.

One day, as I was journaling, a painful realization dawned upon me.

I began noticing a pattern. Whenever I received significant praise for a class or service, I felt a surge of happiness. Yet during my next journaling session, my mind would lash out at this devotee. As I practiced deeper awareness, I uncovered layers of my mind's speech:

1. ***Vaikari* (external speech):** My mind loudly criticized him, calling him names.
2. ***Madhyama* (internal reasoning):** A quieter voice whispered, "Everyone appreciates you except him. What a rascal he is for failing to recognize your qualities."
3. ***Pashyanti* (intuitive insight):** A deeper realization emerged—it wasn't about him. The root cause was my own desire for fame and honor. My mind was reacting because his disapproval stood in stark contrast to the validation I received from others.

In that moment, Krishna's voice seemed to pierce my heart: *"You speak of humility and renunciation, yet you crave respect and admiration. Look at yourself—you are the one seeking false pride and glory!"*

It was a bitter pill to swallow, but I embraced the truth. Accepting my flaws brought both pain and peace. I realized I wasn't as advanced or deserving of praise as I imagined. This humbling realization left me sober yet deeply connected to Krishna. Though it was painful to confront my pride, I felt safe, loved, and anchored in God's presence.

Through this experience, I understood a spiritual truth: *happiness can lead to misery.*

The *Bhagavad Gita* warns us that wise people do not chase happiness, and that day, I saw why. Happiness often makes us greedy for more pleasure. Greed fuels entitlement—like when I sought approval not just from those I was associated with but even from someone estranged. Entitlement leads to ingratitude, and ingratitude plunges us into needless suffering.

This creates a vicious cycle: the more we suffer, the more we seek happiness, trapping ourselves in an endless loop of desire and dissatisfaction.

To break this cycle, we must shift our focus. Instead of chasing happiness, let us seek *gratitude.* Gratitude anchors us in contentment and frees us from the endless pursuit of fleeting pleasures.

However, there is a higher form of happiness—spiritual happiness born of purified emotions. We will explore this energy of emotions in the next chapter.

For now, let us focus on the practical steps to writing a gratitude journal that can lead to spiritual fulfillment.

Four steps to a gratitude journal

Many people write gratitude journals but often find that the practice becomes mechanical or dull. How can we truly unlock the transformative power of gratitude through journaling? Here is a four-step process to guide you:

Step 1: Random list to recognize God

Start by taking a pen and paper and writing down what you're grateful for. In the next five minutes, jot down a random list of events, experiences, or blessings that come to mind. Examples could include:

1. A delicious breakfast.
2. My mother's love.

3. The guidance of my grandparents during my formative years.
4. Time spent studying *Śrīmad Bhāgavatam* for two hours.

Good health.

The key here is to focus on things beyond your control or personal effort—blessings that came from someone else or a higher power. This step helps you acknowledge and recognize God or a power beyond yourself as the source of these gifts.

Step 2: From general to specific gratitude

We often say, "Thank you for everything," in passing. But what does "everything" mean? Gratitude becomes meaningful when we shift from vague expressions to specific instances of thankfulness.

When we identify specific reasons for gratitude, we begin to immerse ourselves in the energy of thankfulness. It is one thing to *say* "Thank you," but another to truly *mean* it. And the deepest expression of gratitude comes when we begin to *live* it through service and reciprocation.

The *Śrīmad Bhāgavatam* provides a beautiful example in the prayers of Kuntidevi. As Krishna prepared to leave after the Kurukshetra War, she thanked Him not vaguely but for specific instances of His protection over the years: saving Bhima from poison, protecting her family from demons, and most recently, shielding her great-grandson from a nuclear weapon (*Śrīmad Bhāgavatam* 1.8.23–24). Kuntidevi shows us the power of moving from general gratitude to specific thankfulness.

In my journaling workshops, participants create gratitude lists that range from 15 to 50 items. These often include:

- Thanking the sun for rising daily
- Appreciation for the municipality supplying clean water
- Gratitude for a neighbor who helps educate underprivileged children, reducing local disturbances

While rewarding, this step can become repetitive or stale over time. That's why the next step introduces an essential element—*fresh gratitude.*

Step 3: Fresh gratitude

Review your gratitude list and highlight a few items for special focus—things that have occurred in the last 24 hours, a week, or even just yesterday. This step encourages mindfulness of recent blessings.

Many of us are conditioned to notice gaps or problems in our lives. Focusing on "fresh gratitude" rewires us to see the good. Even the act of *searching* for something to be thankful for cultivates happiness.

For instance, I ask workshop participants whether they would prefer to *be* a billionaire or simply *feel* like one. Most initially choose the former, but I remind them: when you feel rich, you experience the joy of wealth without the anxieties of taxes or theft. Gratitude creates that sense of wealth—numerous studies show that a simple five-minute gratitude practice has the same emotional impact as hearing your salary has doubled.

This step helps you stay present and recognize God's continuous blessings in your life.

Step 4: Answer the *"Why"* of gratitude

After identifying specific and fresh reasons for gratitude, take it a step further: answer *why* you're grateful for each item.

For example: "I thank God for today's breakfast of *bhelpuri* and *idlis*." This gratitude is specific (*bhelpuri and idlis*) and fresh (*today*). But to deepen the experience, ask *why* this made you grateful.

Your answer might be as simple as, "Because I love good food; I guess I'm a foodie." While this isn't overtly spiritual, it is honest. Gratitude journaling is a process of authenticity, allowing us to acknowledge our desires while connecting with God.

Asking *"why"* helps us delve deeper into our experiences. Over time, this practice can shift from acknowledging material comforts to recognizing spiritual blessings. For instance, I once thanked God for inspiring a friend to prepare a delicious meal. When asked if this was "mundane," I replied, "It's better to remember God for ordinary things than to forget Him in pursuit of extraordinary ones."

Gratitude, though transformative, can initially feel self-centered—it focuses on *my* good experiences, *my* happiness, *my* blessings. To transcend this, we must rise beyond merely saying "Thank you" or even meaning it. True gratitude is *living* it—expressing our thankfulness by serving others.

This brings us to the next stage: *the blessing journal*, where we pray for and express gratitude for others.

7. The blessing journal: Expanding the heart beyond self

We often overthink our own problems, overwhelmed by the endless challenges in our lives. But when we turn our attention outward through a *blessing journal*, something magical happens. Instead of dwelling on ourselves, we begin to think about others—how they might find happiness, how their problems could be resolved. Suddenly, life is not just about *me*.

It is like being a frog in the well of our own mind, unaware of the vast ocean of humanity outside. Many people face struggles far greater than ours. If only we could help them in some small way, even through silent prayers, we might find our own overthinking dissolve into something far more meaningful.

How to start a blessing journal

1. **Write a name:** Begin with someone you know—a friend, a colleague, a family member, or even an acquaintance facing challenges. For example:
   - A friend struggling with their health
   - A neighbor facing financial difficulties
   - A coworker experiencing loss
2. **Add six common words:** For every name, write the following phrase: "Krishna, please, if You so desire." This creates a consistent foundation for your prayers, acknowledging that the ultimate blessings come from God.
3. **Write a specific prayer:** Add a heartfelt prayer for that person. Here is what a blessing journal entry might look like:
   - *Paavani and Achintya*: Krishna, please, if You so desire, let both children be safe, healthy, and happy. Help them navigate their turbulent teenage years with gratitude and trust in their parents.
   - *Paresh*: Krishna, please, if You so desire, let him find

a job soon. He's exhausted his savings after losing his previous job over a year ago. Please protect and support him.

- *Nitin and Madhavi*: Krishna, please, if You so desire, help them bear the pain of losing their daughter Riya in an accident. She was only five. Your plans are beyond comprehension, but their grief is real. Please comfort and heal their broken hearts.

Expanding beyond the self

It is natural to pray for our own family and close circle. But what about the wider world? Most of us know at least 50 people—friends, acquaintances, or coworkers. Offering prayers for just two or three of them each day can gradually expand our hearts like a blossoming lotus, spreading the fragrance of love and goodwill.

However, be mindful that self-centered desires don't creep into your prayers. I discovered this the hard way when I wrote:

Yogesh: Krishna, please, if You so desire, let him realize that I am a nice person and let him appreciate my qualities.

I laughed when I realized this was less about Yogesh and more about *me*! Despite such slip-ups, the blessing journal has been transformative.

A journey of love and joy

During a month-long daily blessing journal practice, I prayed for over five people each day. One morning, during temple prayers, I experienced something extraordinary. As an ashram colleague offered *aarti* to the deities, I felt an overwhelming surge of affection for him. His wonderful qualities filled my heart, and my eyes welled up with tears. Not wanting to draw attention, I stepped outside.

There, I saw a young boy running an errand, and again, my heart overflowed with good wishes: *"Oh Lord, if I have done any good in life, let all those blessings go to him."*

I marveled at the love I felt for everyone I encountered that day—children, strangers, devotees. For a moment, the world felt beautiful, pure, and deeply connected to God. I realized this must be a glimpse into the heart of great souls who experience boundless love and compassion for all beings.

Of course, my mind soon returned to its usual judgments and grievances. But that day, I caught a fleeting glimpse of divine love.

Silent bonds of love

One of the best aspects of the blessing journal is that your prayers remain private. Yet those you pray for often sense this silent energy, creating a natural and unspoken bond. Imagine a world where everyone prayed for one another—envy would give way to love, and abundance would replace scarcity.

I once experienced this while traveling from London to Paris with a youth group. Among the group was Suzanne, a new member who had joined at the last minute. I was skeptical about her presence, worrying that she wouldn't connect with the week-long *Ramayana* classes I was scheduled to deliver.

Feeling helpless, I turned to my blessing journal:

Suzanne: Krishna, please, if You so desire, let her not feel lost during the trip.

Suzanne: Krishna, please, if You so desire, let her develop an attraction for You and Your teachings.

By the end of the trip, Suzanne approached me, her face beaming. Dressed in a sari, she shared how much she loved the *Ramayana*, particularly Lord Rama, Mother Sita, and Hanuman. Her words filled me with immense gratitude. Though we never met again, I felt a spiritual bond with her and saw first-hand how the Lord's mercy had touched her heart.

Blessing journal: A blessing for yourself

The beauty of the blessing journal is that it often benefits you more than the person you are praying for. Who are we to offer blessings to others? God may smile at our attempt, yet He reciprocates by filling our hearts with love and happiness.

Through the blessing journal, we learn to look beyond ourselves, cultivating compassion and connection with others. And in doing so, we take one step closer to making the world a more loving and beautiful place.

I have often heard a lackluster response to journaling exercises: "But I don't feel grateful. I don't feel it in my spiritual practices. It all seems like a drag."

How can we make every day of our lives feel refreshing? How can we cultivate love and happiness that overflow from the heart? What will it take to finally silence overthinking and instead experience lasting joy?

The answer lies in understanding and harnessing the *energy of emotions*—the focus of the next and final chapter of this book.

Part E

Energy

CHAPTER 5

Energy

> *"A person who is not disturbed by the incessant flow of desires—that enter like rivers into the ocean, which is ever being filled but is always still—can alone achieve peace, and not the man who strives to satisfy such desires."*
>
> —*The Bhagavad Gita* (2.70)

Imagine if Virat Kohli or Sachin Tendulkar, at the peak of their cricketing careers, had decided to switch to professional kabaddi or hockey.

Now, consider Michael Jordan, arguably the greatest basketball player of all time, who, at the height of his fame, abruptly retired. If that stunned the sports world, what followed next left everyone even more bewildered. He chose to pursue a career in baseball! For millions of fans who idolized Jordan, one question echoed: Why baseball when he was the best in basketball?

Jordan had just returned from an incredible Olympic run as part of the 1992 U.S. Men's Basketball Team—famously known as the "Dream Team." With legends like Magic Johnson, Larry Bird, Charles Barkley, and eight other future 'Hall of Fame' members, this team was hailed as the greatest sports team ever assembled. Their dominance was so absolute that opponents were more interested in taking photos with them than competing.

The Dream Team won every game effortlessly, scoring over 100 points each time—a feat never achieved before in Olympic history. Their lifestyle off the court was equally extravagant. Staying in a luxury seven-star hotel instead of the Olympic Village, they partied, visited casinos, and basked in their superstardom.

Despite this, Jordan's dedication stood out. While his teammates relaxed, he studied opponents' strengths and weaknesses through game tapes. His unparalleled commitment further endeared him to fans worldwide.

So, why did he retire?

The answer lies in emotion. Jordan's father, who had always dreamed of his son becoming a major league baseball player, had recently passed away. Driven by a deep sense of love and respect for his father, Jordan chose to fulfill his father's wish, even if it meant sacrificing his own passion and potentially his legacy.

The result? Jordan's transition from a basketball genius to an average baseball player was painful for both him and his fans. After two years, he returned to basketball, much to the relief of the sports world.

This story highlights the powerful influence of emotion. Often, our decisions are guided by our hearts, not our heads. While logic may dictate one course of action, emotions can lead us down a different path. This is a universal struggle: the eternal battle between logic and emotion; to find a blend of reason and feeling.

Emotions possess immense power. When we succumb to overthinking, it may seem as though we are analyzing rather than feeling. However, beneath this surface activity lies the reality that our emotional brain has overpowered our rational mind. The rational mind becomes a passive observer, unable to assert itself, while the emotional brain keeps driving our thoughts in circles.

To truly thrive we must harness emotions in ways that uplift rather than diminish our energy. In this chapter we will study how by making conscious choices, strengthening our intelligence, and accessing love of other humans, we can align our emotions with actions that create fulfillment and purpose.

#1 Are We Really Rational?

The raw power of emotion is undeniable. It shapes individuals and societies in ways we often can't fully comprehend.

The word "emotion" itself, derived from the Latin "emovere," means "to move." Anything that stirs us, that compels us to act or react, carries emotional energy. Humans are fundamentally emotional beings, not merely rational ones.

We often pride ourselves on being rational creatures, but the truth is that rationality forms only the tip of the iceberg. Beneath the surface, emotions steer most of our actions and decisions. Even the logic we apply in social interactions often serves to rationalize what we already feel.

This makes it essential to learn how to understand and manage our emotions effectively.

The interplay between logic and emotion—between reason and sentiment—is a constant tug-of-war in our minds.

This dynamic is rooted in the interaction between the brain's prefrontal cortex (the center of rational thought) and the amygdala (the seat of emotional responses). For a deeper dive into this relationship, Daniel Goleman's *Emotional Intelligence* is an excellent resource. He introduced the world to the concept of becoming emotionally strong.

Emotional strength involves self-awareness: understanding our own feelings and thoughts. It is about shifting from reactive, unconscious living to making informed and deliberate choices. An emotionally intelligent person not only navigates their inner world with clarity but also empathizes with others, fostering healthier and more meaningful social connections.

#2 The Importance of Emotional Awareness: A Personal Story

I learned a valuable lesson about the importance of emotional awareness through a rather embarrassing incident.

One day, I received a call from my senior in Delhi. His tone was serious: "I have some bad news for you. I need to talk to you urgently." He explained that he'd be in Mumbai for a few hours before heading to Kolkata and wanted to meet me during that brief window. "Please be available; we cannot postpone this discussion."

When I nervously asked what the issue was, he simply said it was about my future services in the ashram, and that we'd discuss the details in person. Then he hung up.

"What could this serious issue be?" I wondered. My first impulse was to call him back for clarification, but out of respect, I chose not to disturb him. "I'll meet him as requested," I thought. But the phrase 'bad news' kept echoing in my mind.

Soon, my thoughts soared into overthinking, and intense worry gripped me. I imagined the worst: "Maybe he's going to ask me to leave the ashram. Perhaps they think I'm unfit to serve here." Then, indignation replaced my fear: "How dare they think I'm not qualified? I have been nothing but sincere. They are just being narrow-minded and making a mistake!" I spent the next 48 hours consumed by fear, anxiety, and imaginary arguments with myself.

When the day of the meeting arrived, I braced myself for a rebuke. Instead, my senior told me about his deteriorating health, which required him to reduce his responsibilities. He explained that he wanted me to take on his role in congregation development because he trusted me as one of the most responsible and efficient members of the team.

I was stunned. The 'bad news' wasn't about me at all—it was about his health. The 'serious issue' was, in fact, a promotion, a recognition of my dedication to the mission. My mind had completely fabricated a scenario of rejection and failure.

In that moment, everything I had read about emotional awareness, particularly in Daniel Goleman's writings, came alive for me. I also recalled a powerful lesson from Srila Prabhupada: *"First become conscious, and then Krishna conscious."* His words highlighted the importance of becoming aware of our emotional states so we don't let them hijack our minds.

Although I left the meeting feeling elated, my mind soon started spinning again: "How will I manage this new role?

What about the senior monks who are tough to deal with? Will they take offense if I assert my leadership? Maybe I should focus on younger members instead. If others become envious, that's their problem—I'll just concentrate on doing good work."

Again, my thoughts veered into unfounded assumptions about others and even making terrible insinuations—that other monks are spiteful of me. I was yet again riding the mind's chariot.

Today, a few years after that incident, I am able to better recognize my mind's ability to spin yarns or make a mountain out of a molehill. Through practices like breathing exercises and journaling, I now cultivate self-awareness. I now often noticed my *Chanchal* (restless mind) turning into something like Gollum from *The Lord of the Rings*—a scheming, sinister villain plotting to destroy me.

We cannot stop the waves of emotions from crashing into the shores of our minds, but we can learn to ride them. Fear, lust, or anxiety may occasionally surge like a tsunami, but with emotional awareness, we can manage them and channel their energy positively.

Lord Krishna, in the *Bhagavad Gita* (6.6), perfectly captures this:

> *"For him who has conquered the mind, the mind is the best of friends; but for one who has failed to do so, his mind will remain the greatest enemy."*

Often, the mind magnifies a non-existent problem into a crisis. Acting on such irrational fears leads to actions that turn an otherwise safe situation into an actual complication.

Emotional awareness empowers us to prevent such self-sabotage, helping us transform the energy of emotions into a force for growth and strength rather than a source of distress.

I once witnessed a community member demonstrate this extraordinary skill—the ability to transform a completely imaginary problem into a tangible and entirely avoidable predicament.

"I'm really sorry for hurting you. Please forgive me," he said, tears streaming down his face. I stood there, utterly baffled. I couldn't even recall his name, and yet here he was—a middle-aged man—lamenting over what seemed to be a serious dereliction of duty.

I silently wondered who he was and what offense he was referring to. He wiped his tears, took a deep breath, and began recounting an incident that had occurred two months earlier.

It was during our temple festival, where I was part of the crowd management team overseeing over 4,000 visitors. At one point, amidst the commotion, I had apparently asked him to walk faster to make way for a senior couple who needed assistance. I had raised my voice in the process, ensuring the elderly couple could move to the front. He complied immediately.

I couldn't even recall the incident he described, nor could I remember seeing him before or after that festival. He mentioned he was part of our congregation, and as he dropped the names of other community members, it became clear that he was indeed well connected within our circle.

Despite our lack of prior interaction, his overactive mind had transformed a fleeting moment into a significant offense. He suffered over the last two months for nothing.

#3 Creating Positive Emotional Energy – The Three S's

There are many ways to prevent the mind from hijacking our inner peace and we could instead create spiritual and emotional energy within ourselves. While the tools discussed earlier in this book are effective, they are by no means exhaustive. For instance, journaling, as explored in the last chapter, helps release bottled-up emotions. There are other ways to do it as well. It is vital to express our emotions in healthy ways—whether through talking, writing, creating art, or engaging in physical activities like sports or dance.

In this section, we will introduce three additional tools to expand your repertoire for building positive emotional energy:

1. ***Sattva***
2. **Scriptures**
3. **Social blessings**

1. *Sattva*: The mode of goodness

Sattva, one of the three principal modes of nature described in the *Bhagavad Gita*, represents goodness and peace. This energy fosters *awareness*, *acceptance*, and *healthy aspirations*.

In contrast, the other two modes—*rajas* (passion) and *tamas* (ignorance)—can disrupt our inner balance. Overthinking often stems from the dominance of these lower energies. By consciously choosing *sattva*, we can elevate our state of being, embracing clarity and harmony. We will study how to cultivate *sattva* and reduce the influence of *rajas* and *tamas* in our lives.

2. Scriptures: Accessing higher intelligence

Our emotions are often driven by a restless, impulsive mind that behaves like a monkey, jumping from one thought to another. Scriptures offer timeless wisdom and guidance, helping us discern the countless fleeting impulses of the mind for what they truly are—like bubbles on the surface of our consciousness.

By connecting with the teachings of saints and sages and integrating their insights into our lives, we can strengthen our intelligence. A sharper intelligence allows us to control the mind and use it for our growth and well-being, rather than letting it control us.

3. Social blessings: Living beyond oneself

Often, we are trapped in lower energies because we remain self-centered, unable to think beyond our own concerns. This narrow perspective makes us like the proverbial frog in a well—limited in scope and oblivious to the vast ocean of humanity and goodness beyond our small world.

Social blessings come from engaging with others, contributing to their well-being, and drawing inspiration from the collective.

Let us now dive into each of these.

#4 *Sattva* – The Energy of Awareness, Acceptance, and Aspiration

In the pre-dawn hours, many flock to temples, practice yoga, or jog along the ocean, basking in an overall feeling of peace. As the sun rises in the east, it fills the heart with hope and inclines us toward calmness, balance, and clarity. This is *sattva*—the mode of goodness—where emotions like appreciation, gratitude, satisfaction, and kindness take center stage.

As the day progresses, the energy shifts. We rush to work, chase ambitions, negotiate deals, and indulge in sensory thrills. Feelings of excitement, desire, lust, and stimulation dominate, signaling that *rajas*, the mode of passion, has taken control.

By nightfall, fatigue sets in. We may retreat to bed, indulge in unhealthy habits, or wallow in apathy and confusion. This is the domain of *tamas*, the mode of ignorance, characterized by emotions like loneliness, fear, and anger.

The *Bhagavad Gita* teaches that these three modes—*sattva* (goodness), *rajas* (passion), and *tamas* (ignorance)—permeate both our inner world and external reality. Each mode influences every aspect of our life, from food and music to our thoughts, actions, and interactions.

Tapping into *sattva* for daily effectiveness

Our mind often drags us into emotional states shaped by the energies of *tamas* (ignorance), *rajas* (passion), or *sattva* (goodness). Overthinking, for instance, is a hallmark of *tamas*. The *Bhagavad Gita* encourages us to align ourselves predominantly with *sattva*—peaceful and reflective energy. The goal is not to suppress or avoid *rajas* and *tamas* but to use them constructively without letting them control us. A lifestyle rooted in *sattva* ensures that we govern our minds rather than being governed by them.

Sattva energy invites us to slow down, create a pause between life's stimuli and our reactions, and engage our reflective selves. This prevents our impulsive self from derailing our peace and effectiveness.

Let us consider a routine real-life example:

A lesson in choosing *sattva*

After an exhausting day of continuous service, I hit the sack, desperate for rest. Just then, an old friend called, inviting me to join him on an outreach trip to Indian villages, leaving in just five hours.

I was drained and disinterested, so I politely declined. But he persisted, and after nearly an hour of back-and-forth, he finally accepted my refusal and hung up. As I lay there, I realized I had three emotional paths ahead of me:

1. **The *tamas* path:**
   I could dwell on negative thoughts about my friend:
   - "He's selfish; he only calls when he needs something."
   - "No one truly cares for me. Life is unfair and people are selfish."

   These thoughts would have pulled me deeper into *tamas*, leaving me miserable and unmotivated for future endeavors.

2. **The *rajas* path:**
   Alternatively, I could bask in self-importance:
   - "Finally, he recognizes my worth!"
   - "He needed me so desperately; I must be indispensable." This would have inflated my ego and

drawn me into the restless energy of *rajas*, fostering pride and conceit.

3. **The *sattva* path:**
   Instead, I chose to see his call as a divine acknowledgment of my quiet and sincere service. Gratitude filled my heart:
   - "His request is a reminder of the value of my efforts. Perhaps God wants me to reflect on the good I can do."

   This mindset brought peace, clarity, and alignment with my deeper aspirations to serve selflessly. I felt rejuvenated, open to life's next steps, and in harmony with *sattva*.

The transformative power of *sattva*

When we cultivate *sattva*, our emotions become purified, leading to heightened *awareness*, *acceptance*, and alignment with our *aspirations*. This clarity helps us navigate life's challenges with grace and focus. Instead of reacting impulsively or letting our minds spiral into negativity or pride, we find balance and purpose.

The choice is always ours: to sink into *tamas*, revel in *rajas*, or rise into *sattva*.

Case study of Julius Caesar and Brutus

History offers innumerable examples of individuals who succumbed to the relentless energy of uncontrolled emotions, leading to their downfall. At the same time, there are those who rose above their base nature, making choices rooted in clarity and emotional strength.

"Et tu, Brute? Then fall, Caesar!"

These immortal words, written by Shakespeare, capture

the grief and betrayal of Julius Caesar, the dictator of the Roman Republic, as he faced the ultimate treachery at the hands of his trusted friend, Marcus Brutus.

Brutus, a tragic hero, has fascinated the Western world for centuries. He loved his friend Caesar deeply, but his devotion to Rome was paramount. Cassius, a cunning Roman senator and Brutus' brother-in-law, exploited this love for Rome to serve his own agenda. Knowing Brutus' principled nature, Cassius manipulated him by stoking fears that Caesar's ambition endangered the republic.

Blinded by his misplaced sense of duty, Brutus betrayed Caesar, stabbing him to death in one of history's most infamous acts of treachery. Yet this act of "principle" only brought Brutus endless suffering. His wife died by suicide, the corrupt senate he had trusted used and discarded him, and Caesar's ghost haunted him until his tragic end at the Battle of Philippi, where Brutus took his own life.

Brutus allowed the energies of *rajas* (passion) and *tamas* (ignorance) to dominate his mind, clouding his judgment and leading him to ruin.

Sometimes, I wonder if my mind is like Brutus.

We, too, often fall prey to manipulation, buying into others' dreams while abandoning our own. We aspire to be heroes, yet find ourselves entangled in tragedies of our own making. The ghosts of past mistakes haunt us, chaining us to regret and preventing us from living fully. Without realizing it, we may be steering ourselves toward self-destruction.

But there is hope.

Pause and embrace *sattva*

Before succumbing to the chaos of unchecked emotions, *pause* and allow *sattva*—the energy of goodness and clarity—to take the reins. In moments of confusion or temptation, take a deep breath and ask yourself:

- "Where am I right now?"
- "What am I doing?"
- "Why am I doing this?"

This act of mindful reflection fosters *awareness*—the crucial first step toward building emotional strength.

Without taking time to reflect, we risk becoming slaves to fleeting thoughts and feelings, easily swayed by distractions or temptations that derail us from our higher purpose. While passion *(rajas)* has its place, it needs to be guided and tempered by the wisdom and stability of *sattva.*

Brutus serves as a cautionary tale, a reminder of what happens when emotional energies are left unchecked. By cultivating *sattva* in our lives, we can learn to navigate emotions with strength and purpose, avoiding the pitfalls that come from letting *rajas* and *tamas* dominate.

Julius Caesar exemplified an individual who understood his self-worth and refused to let others define it. As a young man, he was kidnapped and held for ransom. Upon discovering that his captors demanded a sum he considered too low, he demanded they increase the ransom, confident in his own value. More impressively, Caesar boldly declared that he would return to punish them. His captors laughed at what they thought was a juvenile boast. But Caesar made good on his word, returning with his troops to crucify every one of them.

This unyielding determination and self-assurance propelled Caesar to greatness, making him a symbol of strength and success. However, even the mighty Caesar was vulnerable to the allure of passion.

The Cleopatra effect

As Caesar's imperial ambitions turned to Egypt, he sought to annex it as a Roman colony. Cleopatra, the fiercely intelligent and ambitious twenty-one-year-old Egyptian princess, had her own designs on the throne. Banished by her brother, Cleopatra saw Caesar as the key to her restoration. Using her feminine charms, she seduced the fifty-one-year-old Roman general. Caesar, captivated, abandoned his initial plans to annex Egypt and instead restored Cleopatra to power by defeating her brother in battle.

In this moment, Caesar's strength became his vulnerability. His unchecked *rajas* (mode of passion) clouded his judgment, making him a pawn in Cleopatra's grander strategy. She used him, manipulated him, and ultimately left him defeated in more ways than one.

Cleopatra was not Caesar's undoing; his unchecked desires and unbridled ambition were. These same qualities left him vulnerable to his final betrayal. The once-mighty Caesar met a tragic end, stabbed to death by sixty members of the Roman Senate, including his trusted ally, Brutus.

The man who once declared, *"Veni, Vidi, Vici" (I came, I saw, I conquered)*, was ultimately overpowered not by an external enemy, but by the unchecked energies within himself.

The inner battle

Like Caesar, we might conquer external goals—whether it is becoming the CEO, a political leader, or a celebrated artist. But what of our inner world? Are we vigilant enough to guard against our own Cleopatras (uncontrolled desires) and Brutuses (hidden betrayals of ego)?

Without self-awareness and a strategy to regulate our needs and impulses, we risk undoing all our external achievements. Temptations, distractions, and inner rebellion can quietly sabotage our progress.

Ask yourself:

- Are you moving forward in life with clarity, or are unseen forces within you pulling you back?
- Are you conquering your inner battles, or are you a victim of your unchecked passions and ego?

Julius Caesar's life teaches us that greatness lies not only in external conquests but also in mastering the inner world. To truly lead a victorious life, we must overcome the challenges created by an untrained mind, and this necessitates we choose *sattva*—to cultivate awareness, accept ourselves as we are, and, with humility and happiness, work within our limitations. This approach allows us to move forward with principles and values that are in harmony with universal laws. Caesar met his downfall because he failed to accept his own fallibility and lacked internal humility as he pursued his ambitions. Similarly, we must forgive, accept, and approve of ourselves rather than chase an ambition disconnected from our true selves.

Along with improving our self-awareness and accepting our reality, we also need to ensure that our aspirations are rooted in purity and values. This is the third essential value: *aspiration*. By focusing on value-based aspirations, we can not only conquer the rebellious tendencies of the mind, but also discover an inner sense of meaning and contentment.

After Caesar's demise, it was the aspirations of those who followed him that would shape the future. Mark Antony and Octavian, both prominent leaders, sought to rule Rome under the Senate's approval. But once again, Cleopatra, with her seductive charms, ensnared Antony. Blinded by passion, he ignored the Roman people's disapproval and indulged in lavish indulgence, weakening himself both politically and personally.

As Antony's love for Cleopatra grew stronger, his focus shifted away from Rome's interests. Eventually, Octavian, backed by the Senate, declared war on Cleopatra. Former allies, Antony and Octavian, were now enemies. Antony, desperate to protect Cleopatra, left his army behind and pursued her, only to be deceived by Cleopatra's message of her death. Consumed by grief, Antony took his own life. Here, *rajas* (passion) and *tamas* (ignorance) led to disastrous consequences.

When Octavian entered Egypt, Cleopatra tried to seduce him as well. However, Octavian, driven by his aspirations and grounded in reality, resisted her charms. With awareness and acceptance of his larger responsibilities—Rome's interests—he remained steadfast, ultimately bringing Cleopatra to her downfall. Realizing she had lost her power, Cleopatra took her own life.

Octavian, now proclaimed as Octavian Augustus, the first

Roman Emperor, ruled Rome for 41 years, leading it into an era of peace and prosperity. He learned from the mistakes of Caesar and Antony, focusing on his values and aspirations, and expanded the Roman Empire, achieving great success.

Every individual can choose to be like Octavian—handling temptations and distractions with care and alertness. Cleopatra had every right to pursue her ambitions, but Antony and Caesar were responsible for their own choices. Similarly, we cannot blame the mind for its nature. The mind will be what it is, but it is up to us to avoid being controlled by its dangerous tendencies while still keeping it content.

The mind is an inseparable part of our being for as long as we live, and so it is wise to learn how to negotiate with it. The key to managing the mind effectively is to tie it to a higher purpose. The more we are connected to our true aspirations, as Octavian was, the less we will be subject to the mind's tantrums.

Life is short, and time slips away constantly. To make the most of it, we must cultivate higher aspirations that transcend the trivial demands of the mind.

These three values form the *brahmastra*, the ultimate weapon to neutralize the overthinking mind. A lifestyle rooted in *sattva* helps us cultivate and sustain these values.

Rising early, taking time for reflection, yoga, or exercise, maintaining moderation in eating, drinking, and sleeping, and spending quality time with loved ones—these practices help us cultivate *sattva*. For a deeper understanding, the 14th, 17th, and 18th chapters of the *Bhagavad Gita* provide a comprehensive explanation of the three modes of nature.

Navigating and transcending the three modes

Sattva serves as the launchpad for those seeking *shuddha sattva* (pure goodness), the spiritual energy that transcends all three modes. In this state, one experiences emotions beyond the mind's fabrications—emotions rooted in divine love and connection. Practices in Bhakti-Yoga that include deity worship, chanting, and visiting sacred places elevate one's consciousness to this spiritual plane. For a plane to soar into the sky, it must first take off from the stable runway of *sattva*.

One evening, I sat peacefully in a garden when an elderly acquaintance joined me. Moments later, he broke wind unapologetically, and the stench was unbearable. He continued to converse nonchalantly, lifting his left butt intermittently to release the suppressed gas he carried inside. I was aghast. I cringed, swore, and hauled him to death in my mind. I was fully enveloped by *tamas*, and ironically, in a picturesque garden.

After he left, I felt relief, but soon a young couple sat nearby, lost in each other's embrace. The strong perfume they put on assaulted my nostrils and pulled me into *rajas*. It was stimulation, no longer suffering, but still far from peace.

I wandered the garden and stumbled upon freshly watered rose bushes. The mingling fragrances of earth, water, and flowers wrapped my consciousness. This was *sattva*—natural, pleasing, and deeply satisfying. I stood still, inhaling deeply, allowing this pure energy to penetrate my being.

Later that night, I returned to the ashram, reflecting on the journey from *tamas* (suffering) to *rajas* (stimulation) to *sattva* (satisfaction).

The fourth stage: Shelter in pure goodness

The next morning, I awoke early and attended the temple's morning prayers. The priest blew the conch shell, and the curtains opened to reveal the deities, Radha and Krishna, adorned in fresh garlands. The serene atmosphere and divine fragrance of garlands filled my senses and soul. Tears streamed down my face as I felt a sense of spiritual love and belonging—a divine union beyond words or emotions. This was shelter-*shuddha sattva*, the shelter of spiritual consciousness.

In less than twelve hours, I had traversed the entire spectrum—from suffering to stimulation to satisfaction and, finally, to shelter.

#5 Scriptures - Providing 'Out-of-the-Box' Remedies

Both of them screamed in agony. Rajesh and Ramesh tossed and turned in their beds, while other patients and visitors in the ward looked on with compassion. To a casual observer, they both seemed equally miserable. However, Rajesh's condition has been diagnosed, and he is aware that a systematic treatment plan has begun. In a few weeks, he will be back on his feet and ready to go home. Ramesh's disease, on the other hand, remains a mystery, and all the medications he's receiving are experimental. At this moment, it seems they are both suffering equally, but Rajesh is in a far better position than Ramesh. Knowing what ails you and understanding how you can help yourself is empowering.

A spiritual practitioner and a materially absorbed person

may both face relationship issues, business losses, poor health, and various calamities. To the average observer, both are suffering in the same way—whether you are Krishna-conscious or not, the unrelenting material energy affects everyone alike. However, a Bhakti-Yoga practitioner has a distinct advantage. Each day, they spend time hearing or studying ancient scriptures, and these timeless words of wisdom, when received with an open heart, reveal the nature of the material world, the different types of miseries we face, and the solutions to end suffering.

In the life of a *Hare Krishna* devotee, two things occur simultaneously: the practice of Bhakti and the struggles of the world. When the anguish of life makes you want to scream aloud, your neighbors may believe that spiritual life hasn't really helped you. They might claim that, unlike you, they haven't practiced Bhakti, yet they suffer just as much. So, they ask, why bother with Krishna consciousness at all? What they don't realize, however, is that while you may be suffering externally like them, internally you are like Rajesh—aware of what is happening, understanding why you are suffering, knowing where you are headed, and recognizing what you need to do. This awareness gives you a sense of spiritual energy, a power that your friends and colleagues lack.

Are these scriptures merely mythology?

There is far more to the *Ramayana*, the *Mahabharata*, the *Bhagavad Gita*, the *Śrīmad Bhāgavatam*, and the *Upanishads* than meets the eye. These ancient texts are not just stories or folklore, they offer insights that have stood the test of time. Here are five examples from these scriptures that prove these are not simply tales for children or "grandmother's stories." In fact, these are just the tip of the iceberg.

1. **The growth of a child in the womb:** How could mythological texts describe the growth of a child in the womb with such astounding accuracy? In the *Śrīmad Bhāgavatam*, which even the most dismissive scholars admit is at least two thousand years old, the third canto, 30th chapter, gives vivid descriptions of the development of an embryo. These descriptions are remarkably similar to what modern embryology, with all its sophisticated scientific tools, explains today.
2. **Animal behavior:** The *Ramayana* begins with sage Valmiki cursing a hunter for killing a male Krauncha bird (Sarus Crane). Valmiki is distraught because he had just taught his students that the female Krauncha is fiercely loyal to her mate and never accepts another partner once bonded. Modern ornithology, the branch of zoology that studies birds, confirms this behavior of the female Sarus. What Valmiki observed in nature thousands of years ago has been verified by science today.
3. **Practical wisdom:** In the *Mahabharata*, during a grueling exchange with *Yaksha*, Yudhishthira is asked which man is truly happy. He responds that a person is happy when three conditions are met: their place of work is close to home, they are free from loans or liabilities, and they have hot food to eat. This practical answer, given five thousand years ago, remains as relevant today as it was then.
4. **Cultural references:** In the *Ramayana*, Bharat scolds his mother Kaikeyi for her decision to send Rama into exile

and secure the throne for herself and her son. He reminds her that in her homeland—what is now modern-day Ukraine or Russia—peacocks are governed by a leader, the oldest peacock, who has a distinctive crest. Bharat argues that this law of leadership is reflected in nature, and her actions in denying Rama the throne are a grave mistake. Historical and cultural evidence from Russian traditions, including 11th-century peacock motifs in clothing and artwork, validates this ancient wisdom.

5. **Prophecy:** The scriptures contain accurate predictions of events and personalities that would appear in the future. For example, the arrival of Chaitanya Mahaprabhu, who lived 550 years ago, is mentioned in both the *Mahabharata* (127.92.75) and *Śrīmad Bhāgavatam* (11.5.32) thousands of years before his birth. Other personalities predicted in the *Śrīmad Bhāgavatam* include Buddha (1.3.24), Chanakya (12.1.11), and the great rulers Chandragupta and Emperor Ashoka (12.1.12).

A genuine question that might arise in your mind is: "If I choose to read scriptures, how will they solve my everyday problems? My life feels overwhelming, and the *Ramayana* and *Bhagavad Gita* are ancient texts. While they may offer fascinating stories and valuable lessons, how can they help me as I navigate my daily struggles?"

How do scriptures give out-of-the-box remedies?

When you feel helpless or frustrated, continuing your daily spiritual practices and connecting with the scriptures will bring unexpected assistance.

This story from the *Ramayana* illustrates the principle beautifully:

The monkey soldiers of Lord Rama were despondent at their failure to find Mother Sita, and in their despair, they decided to end their lives. They gathered on the banks of the Indian Ocean, resolute in their determination. Nearby, a giant vulture named Sampati took notice of this news. Eight thousand years ago, he had burned his wings when he tried to fly too close to the sun. This daring feat not only left him struggling for food but also caused him to fall thousands of miles away from his brother Jatayu. Without wings, Sampati lived a solitary life and was filled with frustration. He considered ending his life, but a wise sage, Chandrama, intervened. The sage predicted that Sampati would one day serve the Supreme Personality of Godhead in a meaningful way and advised him to wait for that moment.

Meanwhile, the *vanaras*—monkey soldiers—had given up their search for Sita. They had exceeded their time limit by two weeks. Their leader, Sugriva, had given them four weeks to find Sita and return to their capital, Kishkinda. Lord Rama had even given Hanuman a special ring to deliver to Sita, assuring her that He and Lakshmana would soon rescue her from Ravana. After six weeks of intense searching, the *vanaras* were still clueless about Ravana's whereabouts, and as their hope faded, they decided to fast unto death. This was, in fact, good news for Sampati, as he would no longer have to search for food.

In their despair, the *vanaras* spontaneously began singing Lord Rama's glories, as their mission in life was to serve Him. They sang and chanted His praises loudly, even though they had not yet fulfilled their task. Sampati overheard their songs and waited patiently, listening carefully. The monkeys spoke of Rama's activities—His birth, His marriage, His banishment to the forest, and His journey up to that point.

Suddenly, at the mention of Jatayu's sacrifice, Sampati's ears perked up. He cried out, "Who is chanting my beloved brother Jatayu's glories? What happened to him? Tell me everything!"

The *vanaras* were surprised to see Sampati, now wingless, and explained what had happened to Jatayu. Sampati, overwhelmed with emotion, wept as he remembered his brother's heroic sacrifice in the service of Lord Rama. Filled with pride, he offered oblations to Jatayu's soul and inquired why the monkeys were planning to die. When they told him about their struggle, Sampati revealed, "I know where Ravana has taken Sita. I cannot fly, but my eyesight is sharp. Eight hundred miles from here, in Lanka, Ravana has imprisoned her."

The *vanaras* were overjoyed. What had seemed like a hopeless search now became a hopeful endeavor.

This story from the *Ramayana* teaches that when life presents confusing challenges and solutions seem out of reach, continue your daily practice of hearing and chanting. You might be surprised at how life can offer 'out-of-the-box' remedy for your situation.

"Get out of your head and spend time in the Lord's space," my mentor in the ashram often told me, especially when I am struggling with challenges. He explained that we tend to live in the "I" space—where our worries, ideas, solutions, and problems consume our minds. But when we make time to live in God's or Krishna's space, we enter a realm of divine possibilities.

In simple terms, this means: take a break from thinking about your problems and spend time hearing and chanting transcendental subjects. This practice helps you connect to a dimension beyond your intelligence, allowing the universe to reveal solutions. There is an infinitely superior force above us, and when we attract its grace, things fall into place, and missing pieces of the puzzle fit together.

The *vanaras*, despite their best efforts, could not find Sita, and their search seemed hopeless. They were dejected, even considering suicide. But their deep love for the Lord, expressed through sincere hearing and chanting, became their salvation.

Srila Prabhupada's books and the vast collection of Krishna-consciousness lectures available online are a great blessing for sincere practitioners. A daily practice of hearing and chanting is a declaration to the universe that we want to live in the Lord's space and receive His grace.

We are small in the face of life's complexities. The more we struggle with it, the deeper we get entangled. But when we choose to hear transcendental sound vibrations, we live in the Lord's presence.

Of course, devotees do work to solve their daily challenges and take responsibility for their lives. However, spending quality time for spiritual activities helps refine our internal receptors, enabling us to access the solutions that God offers us. And that wisdom, far superior to our mental wrangling, is what modern thinkers might call "universal intelligence" or "cosmic consciousness."

Two types of intelligence

There are two types of intelligence: the one we possess as individuals, and the other, known as "cosmic" or "universal" intelligence. In Sanskrit, this is called *mahat tattva,* which encompasses divine or spiritual intelligence, often described as being cloud-like in nature. All the wisdom we encounter in this world is a subset of the vast, spiritual intelligence that resides in the universe.

The intelligence we possess as individuals allows us to make decisions like saying "no" to sugar, memorizing facts, processing information, and making wise choices. This intelligence helps us control our minds (our lower selves). However, despite its potential, our personal intelligence often fails to protect us from our own minds. Rather than guiding us, it sometimes becomes the mind's lawyer—justifying its whims and desires. Over time, this intelligence can become corrupted, losing its sharpness and failing to help us cut through illusions, distractions, and temptations.

To navigate life's complexities, we need to tap into a higher intelligence. The more we open ourselves to the scriptures, allowing their wisdom and divine sound to influence us, the stronger our intelligence becomes, aligning more closely with spiritual reality. We become emotionally resilient and better at saying "no" to negative influences, including overthinking.

Moreover, the compassionate Lord tenderly holds our hands and guides us on our spiritual journey through His words in the scriptures.

Scriptures cure emotional addiction and overthinking

The *Katha Upanishad*, one of the principal Vedic texts, compares the human body to a chariot. The mind is likened to the reins, and intelligence to the driver who controls the horses—representing the senses. As we study scriptures like the *Ramayana*, the *Bhagavad Gita*, or the *Śrīmad Bhāgavatam*, the driver (intelligence) is nourished and strengthened, allowing them to navigate the chariot through the maze of self-obsessive thinking. On a deeper level, these scriptures address the root cause of overthinking—emotional addiction.

Emotional addiction often begins with a seemingly harmless event. For example, you become extremely angry at your child one morning. This anger triggers the release of hormones like cortisol and adrenaline from the adrenal glands. These chemicals spread through your body, creating a feeling of discomfort because they are foreign to the body's natural state. A few days later, the mind becomes angry again due to another event, and once more, the body experiences the same chemical response. Over time, this creates a feedback loop where the body becomes accustomed to these negative emotions.

The first drink or cigarette might be uncomfortable for an addict, but eventually, they become hooked to the chemicals their bodies produce. Similarly, the body, through this feedback loop, starts demanding these anger-related hormones, and the brain justifies it, reinforcing the emotional addiction. This is why some people find themselves perpetually angry, anxious, or caught in other negative emotions—because their body has become addicted to them.

The solution to this is the three S's discussed in this chapter, which help us consciously choose positive emotions. This, in turn, leads to the body becoming addicted to positive emotions. Scriptures play a pivotal role in this process. They strengthen the prefrontal cortex, our higher brain, which helps us regulate emotions. Without using the frontal lobes, we are driven by the amygdala, the emotional and impulsive part of the brain. The amygdala triggers a fight-or-flight response, often leading us to overreact emotionally, even to insignificant fears.

For example, a woman was assaulted as a child and there was coffee brewing nearby. Years later, she may experience fear when she smells coffee, because the amygdala associates that scent with the trauma. However, by activating the prefrontal cortex, she can logically override the emotional response. Regular study of scriptures helps in the cognitive processing of emotions and strengthens the thinking brain.

Through attentive spiritual practice, the brain undergoes rewiring. We may be habituated to certain neural pathways, but by engaging with the scriptures, we begin to create new paths. These sacred texts stir our hearts with the emotions of Hanuman, Krishna, Sita, Rama, Arjuna, and others, teaching us healthy human values and helping us recreate a spiritual reality. As we do this, the body produces positive hormones like serotonin and oxytocin.

In almost all ISKCON temples worldwide, there is a one-hour scripture class every morning. Spiritual students humbly listen to the words of the *Śrīmad Bhāgavatam*, allowing them to purify their consciousness. It is a daily practice that may not provide instant solutions or emotional stimulation, and it may not directly address personal issues. Yet this culture of listening adds positive, spiritual substance to the subconscious mind. The more attentive we are, the more we attract positive emotions to govern our state of being.

#6 Social Blessings – The Energy of Appreciation

On November 19, 2023, while a billion hearts mourned, Rahul Lohar and Dev Ranjan Das, overwhelmed by grief, decided to end their lives. India's tragic loss to Australia in the World Cup finals, after a dramatic and near-perfect winning streak, shattered the nation's hopes. For these two young men, life felt unbearable; they saw no purpose in living after their heroes let them down at the finish line. Instead of celebrating the joy the team had brought to cricket fans over the past month with their extraordinary talent and skills, Rahul and Dev were consumed by the pain of that single defeat.

At the same time, forty-one workers were trapped in a tunnel in Uttarakhand. The nation united in desperation, hoping for their rescue. An engineering team, including two Australian experts, worked tirelessly, and after much effort, all the workers were saved. Citizens prayed fervently for a victory of the combined Indian and Australian teams, and when the workers emerged from the tunnel, the entire country cried tears of joy. People celebrated with sweets, and even the Australian Prime Minister joined his Indian counterpart to honor the victory of the human spirit.

The following week, I asked our youth group for their reflections on these two contrasting events. Though the boys and girls had been distraught by the cricket final loss, the news of the rescue filled their hearts with hope, faith, and immense joy. The group unanimously agreed that the cricket loss paled in comparison to the sacred event of saving lives. They felt that rescuing these workers was far more meaningful than winning a cricket match.

Eight billion of us inhabit this planet with millions of differences. We compete, strive, and excel in different aspects of life. Yet our hearts are bound by oneness and love. When provoked, evolved individuals allow their inherent goodness to prevail over their base instincts. As the most advanced species, it is natural for us to be driven by abundance and kindness. We crave love, both to receive and give, and when we embrace this, the battles of one-upmanship and competitive victories seem insignificant. It is tragic that Rahul and Dev deprived themselves of the happiness that came from giving love, kindness, and service to others. Instead, they allowed the destructive pursuit of their own thrill or gratification to overwhelm them.

When we focus solely on our own happiness, the idea of tapping into the power of blessings or enjoying others' happiness can seem distant and unattainable. But deep down, this is what we as human beings are meant to do—we naturally rejoice in giving love. The Vedic aphorism "*Sarve jana sukhino bhavantu*" (Let all living entities be happy) captures our inherent goodness. The *Śrīmad Bhāgavatam* also emphasizes compassion as a virtue for all humans to nurture:

> *"May there be good fortune throughout the universe, and may all envious persons be pacified. May all living entities become calm by practicing Bhakti-yoga, for by accepting devotional service, they will think of each other's welfare. Therefore, let us all engage in the service of the supreme transcendence, Lord Sri Krishna, and always remain absorbed in thought of Him."* (*Śrīmad Bhāgavatam 5.18.9*)

Two days after the World Cup finals, I was amused to see photos and videos of wild celebrations for Australia's victory in the streets of Dhaka and Karachi. These celebrations went viral, and the joy on the faces of Pakistani and Bangladeshi men could easily have led one to believe that either of those nations had won the World Cup. Initially, I thought these cities must have die-hard Aussie fans, but soon it dawned on me—this happiness was fueled by pure envy. The misery of Indian fans was, for them, a cause for celebration. This is the material world.

Tapping the power of blessings

Many of us are aware that we need blessings from various sources. But how many of us truly understand that we also need to wish good and send blessings to others? Despite our humility, we often fail to realize the profound impact that praying for others can have on our own lives.

When we sincerely wish well for others or celebrate their happiness, our own satisfaction multiplies exponentially. Srila Prabhupada beautifully explains this in a prayer he composed while traveling to America for the first time:

> *"By his strong desire, the Holy Name of Lord Gauranga will spread throughout all the countries of the Western world. In all*

> *the cities, towns, and villages on the earth, from all the oceans, seas, rivers, and streams, everyone will chant the Holy Name of Krishna. As the vast mercy of Sri Chaitanya Mahaprabhu conquers all directions, a flood of transcendental ecstasy will certainly cover the land. When all the sinful, miserable living entities become happy, the Vaishnavas' desire is then fulfilled."*

When Srila Prabhupada wrote this song, he was a seventy-one-year-old man on a cargo ship, battling two heart attacks and sea sickness, on his way to the U.S. to carry out the mission his spiritual master had entrusted to him decades earlier: to preach the universal message of India's wisdom to the English-speaking world. One might feel concerned for Srila Prabhupada and his mission—it didn't make logical sense to teach Krishna consciousness to Westerners when he had no support, no money, and no clear plan. Srila Prabhupada himself later admitted that during his initial struggles, he would sometimes wander aimlessly through the streets of New York, unsure of how things would unfold to spread Krishna consciousness. But what Srila Prabhupada did carry with him was his compassion and love for others.

A few years earlier, Srila Prabhupada had been distributing his *Back to Godhead* journals in the streets of Delhi. He encountered many cynical individuals who showed little interest in his urgent plea to embrace Krishna consciousness. Undeterred, he continued his preaching. His only desire was for people to connect with Krishna and experience spiritual happiness. His eagerness to share this knowledge kept him so absorbed that he often skipped meals. Despite facing financial challenges, he left no stone unturned in his efforts to spread Krishna consciousness. His own comfort was never a consideration—people's suffering caused him deep pain, and his only wish was to see them happy. During this time, he was gored by a bull in the streets of old Delhi, and once, he collapsed from a heat stroke. A well-wisher picked him up and gave him shelter. But despite these challenges, Srila Prabhupada never thought of his health or happiness—his mission to share the wisdom of Krishna consciousness remained his only focus.

Later, when he began preaching in New York, Srila Prabhupada found himself completely alone. He rented a small apartment, where his typewriter was stolen and a crazy hippie even tried to attack him. Srila Prabhupada endured many insults and the unpredictable behavior of people under the influence of drugs, but he focused on helping them. One young man, despite lacking resources or interest in helping, listened to Srila Prabhupada's teachings on Krishna consciousness. Srila Prabhupada disregarded his disqualifications and gave him everything he had. Anyone who showed even a little interest received Srila Prabhupada's full attention and compassion.

Months later, when he began preaching at 26 Second Avenue, Srila Prabhupada cooked lunch daily for over a dozen young men. Some ate more than a dozen chapatis, others expected him to save food for them because they'd be late from work, and some contributed nothing but took service from Srila Prabhupada. Yet he never complained. He was grateful to serve, ensuring that these young men and women had the opportunity to feel Krishna's love in their hearts.

Srila Prabhupada's daily cooking and his Sunday love feasts became renowned in ISKCON's folklore.

Srila Prabhupada's example for future generations

Steve was one of the young men who began visiting Swamiji's storefront, and he once heard Srila Prabhupada mention in a class that the city of New York had no fresh fruits. Srila Prabhupada went on to say that in India, he would enjoy succulent mangoes. Steve deduced that Swamiji must love mangoes and decided to get some for him the next day. After searching for mangoes everywhere, he finally found just a few in a distant Indian store. The next morning, after class, Steve presented these mangoes to Srila Prabhupada. Srila Prabhupada's face lit up, his eyes widened in delight, and he said, "*Accha*, mango. Wonderful!" Then, rubbing Steve's head affectionately, as a father would his son, he added, "Nice boy." Everyone in the room laughed at this sweet gesture. For a moment, Srila Prabhupada didn't understand why the devotees were laughing. He became serious and said, "Why do you laugh? He brought mangoes, which is a sign of love. This is love."

At first glance, this incident might seem trivial, but years later, during the tenth anniversary celebrations of ISKCON, Srila Prabhupada recalled this moment of receiving a mango from Steve. By then, Steve had become well-known as Satsvarupa das Goswami, a senior sannyasi, and other young men had also risen to leadership roles. Srila Prabhupada, now a world-renowned leader, had appeared on international magazines and prime-time television. Surrounded by hundreds of disciples, with thousands waiting to hear his every word, Srila Prabhupada looked at the cake prepared for the event and said, "Our Satsvarupa das Goswami would get me a mango out of love."

Acknowledging such small, kind acts shows that Krishna consciousness is not some lofty, abstract spirituality. It is rooted in simple, human exchanges of love and affection. This affection arises naturally from a heart filled with deep appreciation for others. Srila Prabhupada truly cared for everyone, seeing each person as a part and parcel of Krishna. He saw himself as a servant of Krishna, eager to offer Krishna's love to all souls, especially those who were conditioned by the material world.

Radhanath Swami writes about a similar personality, Ghanshyam Das, in his memoir *Journey Home*. As a young seeker, Richard (Radhanath Swami) observed Ghanshyam embody compassion and love in a way rarely seen in society. Ghanshyam saw everyone as a devotee or friend of his worshipable deity, Gopijana Vallabh (a form of Krishna). He viewed himself as a servant of the Lord and wished to serve all of Krishna's friends. Whatever food (*rotis*) he had, he fed to Richard. He offered his blanket, place of rest, and food, all in service to Krishna's devotees.

Imbibing this same spirit of love and care, Radhanath Swami emphasized that these qualities should form the foundation of the community he established and now leads in Mumbai. When I joined the monastery, during one of our early classes, Radhanath Swami asked, "How many of us are staying here?" Someone answered, "Forty." Then he asked, "If each of us cared only for ourselves, how many would be caring for us?" We responded, "One." He continued, "Now, if each of us took care of others, how many would be caring for us?" "Thirty-nine," we answered. He smiled and said, "See, even logically, it pays to always live for others." He emphasized this truth with love and clarity.

ISKCON founded on care and love

Many of Srila Prabhupada's early devotees recall with great fondness the personal care he showed them, not only in helping them understand philosophy, but also in attending to their practical needs. He nourished them with good food, helped them find gainful employment, and even assisted in arranging marriages.

Lilavati, a young girl, was once admitted to the hospital due to prolonged illness. When Srila Prabhupada visited the temple, he inquired about her well-being. Upon learning that she was in the hospital, he insisted that all the devotees temporarily halt their services to visit her. When Lilavati saw so many devotees come to her bedside in a joyful, celebratory mood, it uplifted her spirits. She was deeply moved when she learned that it was Srila Prabhupada who had insisted on this simple yet powerful gesture of care.

Another young woman, Sarveshwari, was pregnant. One evening, as Srila Prabhupada was retiring from his program, Sarveshwari brought him a cup of hot milk. Srila Prabhupada noticed she was expecting and paused to inquire about her well-being. He then insisted that she drink the milk she had brought for him. Initially embarrassed, Sarveshwari tried to insist that the milk was for him and that she would take hers later. But Srila Prabhupada insisted she drink it and called upon the temple president to ensure Sarveshwari was well cared for and properly fed.

Through such actions, Srila Prabhupada demonstrated that Krishna consciousness is not merely an abstract philosophy but a practical way of life. It is centered on serving one another in the mood of being the servant of the servant of Krishna's devotees.

Cultivating appreciation at three levels

Extending ourselves for others is not just a formality; it is deeply rooted in appreciation and love.

To awaken the energy of appreciation and love, I conduct an exercise called "Three Levels of Appreciation" during my workshops.

In this exercise, participants pair up and reflect on a person they would like to appreciate for something that person has done for them in their personal lives. In the first round, each participant shares with their partner how their life has been touched by the kindness or inspiration of this person. It is important that the person they choose is someone other than their spiritual master or Srila Prabhupada, and that they are still alive. This is because it is often easier for us to appreciate exalted personalities or those who have passed away, but appreciating those who are still with us is equally important.

For example, if I were your partner, I would share my appreciation for a friend named Mehul. He left his comforts in Mumbai to come help me when I was caring for my mother in my hometown during the COVID-19 pandemic. He helped me find a house to rent, cleaned, bought medicines, and cooked. His support was invaluable during that difficult time. After I finish, you would speak about the person you appreciate, whether it is a family member, neighbor, teacher, or friend.

In the second round, participants appreciate the same person, but with a shift in perspective. This time, you appreciate the person for who they are, independent of what they have done for you. It is as if you no longer exist in this world, and it is only about the person you're appreciating. For instance, in the second round, I would talk about how Mehul is a wonderful man who goes above and beyond for others. He regularly visits the holy town of Gaya to offer oblations to his ancestors, expressing gratitude through traditional rituals. He cooks for his mother every weekend and has been awarded the best employee award multiple times.

In this round, my appreciation is entirely about Mehul—nothing about how he benefited me. This shift opens a higher dimension of happiness, as we begin to acknowledge that there is more to life than just ourselves. We recognize that the world is filled with goodness, regardless of whether we exist to acknowledge it.

By the end of these two rounds, you have not only spoken positively about someone else, but you have also heard the good qualities of another person. The third round is where the exercise reaches a spiritual dimension. Both participants now take the names of the people they appreciated in the previous rounds and reflect on the divinity in them. While in the first two rounds, we focused on the qualities in relation to ourselves and the world, now we see how these qualities are universal—qualities exhibited by great saints or divine personalities in the scriptures.

For example, during the third round, I saw Mehul

displaying qualities reminiscent of Lord Chaitanya, the Supreme Personality of Godhead, who is known as *matra bhakta siromani*—"the greatest devotee of the mother." Lord Chaitanya served and respected His mother deeply. I also reflected on how Srila Prabhupada dedicated his *Krishna Book* to his father, and I began to see Mehul carrying these divine qualities in his actions.

The third round is often an eye-opener. We learn to see the person beyond our immediate reality. Our appreciation of others typically begins with recognizing what they do for us, which is a necessary first step in cultivating a vision of goodness. But in the third round, we rise above our limited perspective to see goodness beyond ourselves, thus connecting with a higher, spiritual reality.

Real-life examples

After one workshop, a man confided in me that during the first round, he was surprised when his partner began appreciating someone from the community whom he personally disliked. Out of politeness, he didn't say anything and continued to listen respectfully to the praise being offered. "I couldn't digest the fact that this person is so good," he said, "but I kept reassuring myself that it is just my partner's experience, it is an exception. I just quietly tolerated it." At the end of the first round, he was relieved it was over. But what he heard in the next round completely shocked him. He learned that the person he had particularly disliked had done incredible, selfless service for many people and was not as bad as he had thought.

The most startling part came in the third round, when he

had to not only hear but also actively search for divinity in this person. As part of the third level of appreciation, he had to recognize how the qualities of this person mirrored those of the Lord and His intimate associates. He returned home that night sober and humbled, realizing he had been wrong in his estimation of this person.

After one particular workshop, a lady shared in front of two hundred people that she now sees her husband with more respect and appreciation. Her husband had a unique gift—an intuitive sense that allowed him to know when his wife would feel uncomfortable in certain social settings. He would suggest that she not attend a particular event, but the lady often ignored his advice and went ahead anyway. Later, things would unfold exactly as he had predicted, but instead of thanking him for his foresight, she would accuse him of "cursing" her attempt to enjoy the event. "But thanks to the workshop," she said gratefully, "I can now see my husband is truly gifted and that he cares for me." I asked her if she could apply the third level of appreciation—could she see divinity in him? Without hesitation, she responded, "Yes, my husband reminds me of Lord Shiva in the fourth canto of the *Śrīmad Bhāgavatam*, who advised his wife, Sati, not to attend her father's party, but she defied his good counsel. I can now see my husband as Lord Shiva." The room erupted in laughter and applause. Her husband, seated at the far end of the hall and an active participant in the workshop, raised his hand and asked for the microphone. "I'm grateful that my wife is finally able to see me as Lord Shiva," he said to the packed room. "But let me confess, I have always seen her as non-different from the fiery Durga."

Overthinking keeps us bound to our own mind and intellect. Worse still, it limits our ability to see the goodness in others. Even when we do appreciate others, we often remain confined to our narrow worldview. The three levels of appreciation are an effective tool to help us rise beyond these limitations and tap into the energy of blessings. In that blessed state, overthinking fades away, and even if we occasionally slip into overthinking, it no longer carries malice; we are able to rise above it and take charge of our lives.

Conclusion

Purifying Overthinking with Spiritual Emotions

"Krishna is never conquered by anyone, but a devotee can conquer Him through devotional service.... One cannot understand Krishna simply by reading Vedic literature. Although all Vedic literature is meant for understanding Krishna, one cannot understand Krishna without being a lover of Krishna."

—Srila Prabhupada {Purport to Chaitanya Charitamrita, *Madhya Lila*, 4.137}

I felt like a batsman returning to the pavilion after scoring a century. I waved my bat in the air, feeling on top of the world.

Every day, I traveled for over two hours in the local trains of Mumbai, selling books as part of our preaching activities. Initially, I would manage to distribute around thirty to forty books in that time. I would show the books to people, explain their contents, answer their questions, and encourage them to buy. Most people ignored me; many took the books but returned them after seeing what they were, some would ponder for a while, and others would take them home. It wasn't easy, but the rewards were fulfilling. When I returned to the temple late in the evening, I felt a deep sense of satisfaction. But today was different—I had distributed more than one hundred books in just two hours. I could hardly believe it.

The next morning, when the scores were announced in the temple hall, devotees were delighted. Many monks congratulated me, saying what I had done was unprecedented. From that point on, whenever I returned from book distribution, devotees gathered around to ask me my score. I consistently maintained over one hundred books, feeling like a champion batsman scoring centuries every time I went out to bat. The thrill and excitement of selling transcendental literature was unlike anything I had ever experienced. I was twenty-six, and my spiritual life in the monastery was beginning to feel deeply fulfilling. I felt content and driven by a missionary zeal. Book distribution brought me immense happiness.

One day, I failed. I tried hard, but after three hours of focused effort, I managed to distribute only twenty-five books. I returned disappointed, but the worst was yet to come. The next morning, during the announcement of scores, a friend approached me and said, "Hmm, your scores have dropped. Are you spaced out these days?" I was taken aback and quickly explained that I had worked very hard, but he seemed unimpressed. That evening, I struggled again, and devotees no longer praised me. Desperation set in as I tried to return to my previous high scores, but nothing seemed to work.

As I showed books to a couple, I silently began to pray to Lord Krishna. "Please Krishna, let them take these books and begin their spiritual journey now," I prayed in my mind even as externally I was preaching to them. The man briefly glanced at the books and then returned them. I hurried to another passenger and silently begged Krishna, "Please Krishna, You are present in his heart as the Super Soul; please awaken his interest in spiritual life." As the man flipped through the books, I continued my intense prayers. Externally, I smiled and stayed calm as people looked at the books, asked questions, or returned them. But internally, I was sincerely praying with every approach.

That evening, I returned exhausted with only thirty-five books. Strangely, as I walked the usual distance from the Grant Road station to the temple, I felt happy. Despite the fact that I had distributed far fewer books than on other days, I felt a sense of peace. A monk asked about my score, and I realized that I was at peace even as I shared my experience. Gone was the anxiety about how others would judge my "performance." Book distribution was no longer just a theatrical show to gain popularity or personal recognition. It had become a sacred service. I felt Krishna conscious and spiritually uplifted. As I had dinner and retired for the night, I also realized that my consciousness was better that day compared to previous days when I had scored over one hundred books.

What had made the difference? It slowly dawned on me—it was my internal mood of prayer. I had approached the service with genuine spiritual emotions, remembering Krishna with love and sincerity, and wishing for the spiritual benefit of others.

This pattern repeated over the following days. As I traveled to the station, I offered prayers to our worshipable deities,

Srila Prabhupada, and my guru. Then, I dedicated myself fully to my service for three hours. When I returned in the evening, I felt happy. A few days later, I again reached a score of over one hundred books. This time, the devotees appreciated me, but I remained grounded. I felt indifferent to the praise. What mattered most was that I had been emotionally connected with Krishna during my service. Whenever I connected with Krishna, I could see I had transcended the need for external validation, and when I didn't feel Krishna's love, I sought the approval of the world outside of me.

#1 The Emotional Strength to Face Suffering

When I shared this experience with my mentor, he affirmed my insights and explained that the essence of Bhakti-Yoga lies in always remembering Krishna with love, and never forgetting Him. He said that when we remember Krishna, we become spiritually happy, and the fame and infamy, as well as the successes and failures of this world, no longer matter. Our experiences transcend material concerns because our mind and heart have connected with the all-pure Krishna through emotions. According to the Vedic scriptures, Krishna is the Supreme Personality of Godhead, and when our mind and intelligence align with Him, we transcend material limitations.

He also shared the example of Queen Kunti, who derived so much transcendental bliss from remembering Krishna that she actually wished calamities would strike her again and again. She preferred the miseries of life because, in those moments, she remembered Krishna and felt an extraordinary sense of love and closeness to Him.

Some years ago, the story of an orphan boy, who had received a nurse's love, became widely known. While playing cricket in a slum, the boy was badly injured and was rushed to a charitable hospital. Screaming in agony, he was lovingly cared for by an elderly nurse who helped him recover. Months later, the boy was back playing with his friends, and as he looked toward the hospital, he wished he could be injured again. His friends were shocked and asked why he would wish for such a painful experience. Didn't he remember how much he had screamed during the accident? With a smile, he replied, "Yes, I know I was in distress, but during that time, I experienced a glimpse of what a mother's love feels like." With tears in his eyes, he continued, "She was so loving and kind. It was worth going through the pain if I could experience her love again."

In the Bhakti-Yoga tradition, saints like Mirabai, Haridas Thakur, Vasudev Dutt, and Tukaram, among many others, endured immense hardships while spreading the Lord's message of love. They never harbored anger toward those who mistreated them; they only wished good for others. This is because they constantly received the love of Krishna, the 'nurse' who nurtured them, and they preferred that experience over any suffering the world could bring.

Many of us face our share of suffering in life, but the situation often worsens because of the way we "horribilize" it in our minds. We ruminate and overthink to the point where the problem seems insurmountable. At such times, Bhakti-Yoga practices, which involve the loving remembrance of

Krishna, enrich our hearts and help us see the problem for what it truly is—a tiny obstacle compared to the immense love of the Lord that continually beckons us. A devotee doesn't tell Krishna how big their problems are; instead, they tell their problems how great Krishna is. Krishna helps us see everything in its proper perspective.

#2 From Intellectual to Emotional Remembrance of God

Overthinking is like a desperate attempt to escape a swamp. The more we flap our hands and legs, the faster we sink. Similarly, the more we overthink, the further the solution seems to slip away from us. Even as Bhakti-Yoga practitioners, many of us fall into the trap of reducing our remembrance of Krishna to an intellectual exercise. We memorize verses, absorb philosophical knowledge, and gather information from the scriptures. We may even engage in debates with agnostics and impersonalists, proving that Krishna is God, that He is all-loving, and that we should surrender to Him. Yet, despite all this knowledge, we could still be victims of overthinking, just as much as someone who knows nothing about Krishna. In fact, we might even end up engaging in harmful actions, driven by a misguided understanding of what is important and what is not. A notorious example is Raman Raghav, a serial killer in Mumbai who bludgeoned at least thirty-five people to death. When caught, he claimed that God had instructed him to kill and that Jesus would forgive him for his actions.

To transition from mental entrapment to meaningful action, we need to shift from an intellectual approach in Bhakti-Yoga to one based on spiritually fulfilling experiences. Instead of just memorizing details about Krishna—where He was born, when He went to Mathura, or His age during the Battle of Kurukshetra—we need to also remember how God has personally helped us or how He has cared for someone we know. When we know all the details about Krishna but fail to personalize His presence in our lives, we are merely falling in love with His "bio-data"—it remains just information. There is more to Krishna than knowing about Him; we need to love Him.

To truly love Krishna, we need to recognize how God has intervened in our lives. I recall a memorial service for a senior lady in our congregation, where different members shared their appreciation of her. Her son spoke at the end, recounting how his mother had been married as a teenager, lived in extreme poverty, and came to Mumbai to educate herself. At first, he shared technical details about her life, which felt like intellectual remembrance. But as he continued, he moved into a deeper emotional space. He described how, at times, his mother ate only once every three days to ensure that her children had enough to eat. As he extolled her selfless love, her impact on the family and community, and the devotional qualities she embodied, his eyes filled with tears of gratitude and affection.

We, too, remember Krishna intellectually, knowing all the details from the *Bhagavad Gita* and being able to recite verses from different chapters to make our points. Yet, to deepen our connection, we must remember how Krishna has personally helped us or those we know. That is how we move from simply knowing Krishna to truly loving Him.

Srila Prabhupada emphasized this in his class on July 1971 in Los Angeles, titled *'Just Learn to Love Krishna'*. While sharing the story of a South Indian Brahmin's emotional connection with Krishna, Srila Prabhupada said, "This is success in Bhakti-Yoga—we need to feel 'Krishna is so nice, Krishna is so kind.'" The context for this class was Srila Prabhupada's explanation of a South Indian man, who was illiterate, yet felt deeply emotional when he attempted to read the *Bhagavad Gita*. When Lord Chaitanya asked him how he could cry while reading the *Gita*, the man explained that he felt Krishna was so loving that He became a charioteer for His devotee Arjuna. The man told Lord Chaitanya that although he was illiterate, he felt deeply connected to Krishna whenever he saw the *Bhagavad Gita*, because he remembered how the Lord became Arjuna's charioteer. Srila Prabhupada repeated the phrase, "Krishna is so nice, Krishna is so kind," several times in this class to underscore the importance of emotionally investing in our relationship with God.

Once, after I quoted this Srila Prabhupada lecture in my own class, twelve-year-old Revati asked me how she could feel "Krishna is so nice, Krishna is so kind" when she couldn't connect to the fact that Krishna drove Arjuna's chariot. I replied that Krishna is also 'driving' her chariot. I asked, "Have you ever been on the road in a car with your parents or friends when you had a narrow escape from a near accident?" She immediately responded, "Yes," and many others in the audience raised their hands, affirming that they had experienced similar close calls. I asked the group, "Who was 'driving' your chariot at that moment?" I explained, "Can't we connect the dots in our lives and recognize that it is Krishna (God) who is orchestrating the course of our lives?" The more we see how God orchestrates the events in our lives, the more we transition from intellectual remembrance to emotional connection with Him.

#3 The Three-Step Journey from Material to Spiritual

We often slip into overthinking because material emotions like anger, lust, envy, fear, and insecurity are too familiar, while spiritual emotions—such as crying in pure love for God or experiencing ecstatic transformations in the body due to separation from the Lord—can seem too fantastical. Spiritual states may feel abstract or distant for many of us. Thus, it is natural for a mind unfamiliar with deeper spiritual truths to resort to overthinking.

The solution to overthinking, and to self-obsessive thoughts in general, is to enter a middle ground of spirituality—a semi-spiritual path where we cultivate emotions of appreciation, gratitude, kindness, and love. These emotions form the foundation of all spiritual states. Anyone experiencing a spiritual high would naturally feel love surging in their heart and deep appreciation for life's blessings. By cultivating these emotional states, we can make our spiritual journey more practical and accessible.

In the previous chapters, we have explored different positive emotions. If we sincerely nurture these emotions, overthinking will fade into the background, a distant memory from a past life. Meanwhile, practices like chanting, meditation, scripture study, and service will spiritualize our positive emotions and help us enter deeper states of Bhakti-Yoga. This is how we evolve both emotionally and spiritually.

There are three steps we can follow to spiritualize our emotional states. The journey begins with appreciation for the simple, daily gifts in life. Next, we deepen our gratitude by reflecting on things that are not immediately apparent. Finally, we learn to appreciate a reality beyond ourselves, recognizing the presence and guidance of the divine in all things.

#4 Applying the Three Steps

While chanting the *Hare Krishna* mantra on beads, you might struggle to emotionally connect with Krishna for various reasons. Perhaps you're new to Bhakti-Yoga practices or find the concept of God as a person unfamiliar. In such moments, while you go through the external motions of chanting and hearing scriptures, try inwardly investing your emotions in gratitude. Begin by remembering someone who has shown you kindness. Reflecting on their selfless love can subtly shift your consciousness toward a spiritual state. After all, any act of genuine love in this world reflects God's universal love for all beings. By recalling such acts with gratitude during chanting, you touch emotions that elevate your mind to a higher plane.

Step 1: Gratitude for daily gifts

Initially, your reflections may be self-centered, focused on the direct kindnesses you have received. That's okay—gratitude, even in its simplest form, expands the heart.

Step 2: Deeper gratitude for subtle experiences

Over time, you will naturally begin to notice subtler blessings. For instance, I once remembered an old incident while giving a class. That spontaneous recollection added a story to my talk, which the audience loved. Later, while filling my gratitude journal, I paused to thank God for "advising" me at just the right moment.

Had I not cultivated a practice of reflection, such gratitude might have slipped my mind. Initially, I would thank God for tangible things like good food or audience appreciation. But over time, I began to perceive deeper, less apparent blessings—ideas that arose unexpectedly, scriptural insights that resonated, or memories of kindness from years ago. These are instances of gratitude for experiences that transcend the senses, helping us move beyond the obvious.

As you grow in gratitude, you will learn to appreciate what lies beyond the surface. This involves recognizing God's hand in subtle, often unseen ways—His "advice," "arrangement," or "allowance" in shaping events and outcomes. These realizations may not come easily at first; the mind might go blank. But with practice, you can learn to see miracles in everyday occurrences—a sudden idea, a chance encounter, or a moment of clarity. Such reflections help us delve deeper into appreciation, cultivating a gratitude that goes beyond the immediate and material.

Step 3: Appreciation beyond self

The third step involves shifting focus from your own life to a reality beyond yourself. Recently, I met an old friend who shared the incredible spiritual journey of Ramesh Babaji, a saintly devotee who has spent decades protecting the sacred mountains of Braj (in Vrindavan) from illegal mining. Listening about his devotional service filled me with joy. Later, in my gratitude journal, I thanked God for the opportunity to hear about such a selfless soul.

But this gratitude also led me to a deeper reflection. I meditated on Ramesh Baba's sixty-two years of unwavering, selfless service. Despite his spiritual exaltation, he refuses to accept disciples, considering himself unqualified. He never solicits funds for his incredible work, depending entirely on the Lord. At this third level, my meditation was not about me at all. It was about the beauty of Ramesh Babaji's devotion—a celebration of God's love manifest in his life.

This kind of appreciation transcends personal worries or joys. It shifts our focus to the Divine, allowing us to marvel at how others embody God's love. By exploring this higher level of gratitude—beyond self-concern—we step closer to spiritual consciousness. And as we combine these deeper meditations with the gratitude we feel for our own experiences, we make steady progress on the path to spiritual awakening.

#5 Goal of This Book - Living with God Always

The goal of this book, like the essence of all Bhakti traditions, is to inspire us to live with God in every moment of our lives.

Just as we turn to loved ones to share our joys and sorrows, we can turn to Krishna with the same intimacy. When we spontaneously remember Krishna or emotionally connect with Him in love, we are living with God, and our lives become spiritual. It doesn't matter if we are monks, warriors, children, or professionals—what matters is where our heart rests. As the *Bhagavad Gita* (8.7) reminds us:

> *"Therefore, Arjuna, always think of Me, and at the same time carry out your duty of fighting. With your activities dedicated to Me and your mind and intelligence fixed on Me, you will attain Me without doubt."*

Ayush, a dear friend, recently shared a transformative experience that beautifully encapsulates this book's message.

It was 1.30 a.m., and Ayush was overwhelmed with anxiety. His CPA exam was just two days away, and the weight of his aspirations, coupled with financial pressure, felt unbearable. He couldn't focus despite studying for ten consecutive late nights. Alone and two thousand miles away from his family, Ayush debated whether to call his wife, Siya, at such an odd hour.

Siya, his best friend and confidante, had always been his rock, and he desperately needed her reassurance. Though he hesitated, the mounting fear drove him to dial her number. After several rings, Siya answered, alarmed by his late-night call. As they spoke for over half an hour, Ayush found solace in her comforting words and love. But just before hanging up, Siya gently said, "Honey, I understand you're going through a lot. But couldn't we have spoken after the kids went to school? You know how hectic mornings are. I could have used some rest."

Ayush immediately apologized, and they ended the call on a positive note. Later, Ayush confided in me, expressing both gratitude and a sobering realization. While he was immensely thankful for Siya's support, he also recognized the inherent limitations of human relationships. "She did her best," he admitted, "but I expected too much. It wasn't her fault—I was just looking for more. And I need to remember that she's human too, with her own challenges and responsibilities."

Then, as if struck by a realization, Ayush picked up his bead bag and smiled. "But I can call Krishna anytime, any day, and He'll never complain about being disturbed."

#6 Discovering God as the Perfect Companion

The following night, when the panic returned, Ayush was better prepared. Instead of calling Siya, he chanted the *Hare Krishna* mantra on his beads. As he chanted, he reflected on his gratitude for Krishna, for Siya, and for the countless blessings in his life. He poured out his worries to Krishna, feeling as though he were speaking to a trusted companion—one who had been with him not just in this life but through all his previous lifetimes and would remain with him in lives to come.

This practice brought him immense peace. That night, he slept soundly. The next day, when Siya called, Ayush was fully present for her, listening empathetically to her concerns and offering thoughtful support. Siya, pleasantly surprised, remarked on his newfound calmness and understanding, even amidst his personal challenges.

Through this experience, Ayush learned a sacred truth: spending time with God not only alleviates our own worries but also enriches our relationships with others. By anchoring his heart in Krishna's love, Ayush found the strength to navigate his anxieties and support those who mattered to him.

This is the essence of living with God. When we cultivate a personal connection with Krishna, we unlock a reservoir of peace, love, and resilience. We learn to approach our challenges with grace and our relationships with selflessness. Life becomes a shared journey with the Divine, and in this companionship, we find fulfillment that surpasses the limitations of this world.

Acknowledgements

My foremost gratitude goes to His Divine Grace Srila A.C. Bhaktivedanta Swami Prabhupada, who taught by his example and teachings, how to practically live a life of meaningful action—the ultimate antidote to overthinking.

My deep thanks to my spiritual master, His Holiness Radhanath Swami, who embodies mindful living and investing spiritual emotions in our relationship with God—the two critical weapons to save us from the overthinking trap.

My sincere appreciation to Govinda Prabhu, Shyamananda Prabhu, Radha Gopinath Prabhu, Sanat Kumar Prabhu, Gauranga Prabhu, Radheshyam Prabhu, Krishna Chandra Prabhu, Madhavananda Prabhu, and Satcitananda Prabhu for their leadership and guidance to thousands of our congregation members—their non-judgmental encouragement helps me and others find a sense of purpose and contribution.

My thanks to His Holiness Bhakti Vijnana Goswami Maharaj. His classes have helped me go deeper into my own spiritual practices and learn practical tools to overcome overthinking.

This book has seen the light of day due to the tireless management of my dear friend, Abhishek, and his wife, Hiral. Shaswat, Shivam, Kumari Gopika, and Pawan helped me with the initial proofreading and editing. My immense gratitude to Surabhi Bharadwaj, Vrushank, Disha, Mohit, and Riya for their timely feedback and help in connecting with the publishers and getting the logistical support to get this book printed.

I thank Deepti Patel for her help in connecting with Jaico Publishing House. My thanks to the editorial team of Jaico for showing faith in my manuscript and taking it up for publication. My sincere thanks to Sri Gokulananda who gave me shelter of his own house in Vrindavan to help me complete the manuscript.

I have learnt from many monks in our ashram as well as from various traditions. My friends, namely, Gauranga Priya dasa, Gaur Gopal dasa, Chaitanya Charan dasa, Sikshastakama dasa, Shivram dasa, Baladeva dasa, Sri Chaitanya dasa, Manohar dasa, Nanda Dulal dasa, Mukunda Mala dasa, Radhesh Lala dasa, Shadbhuj dasa, Vraja Chandra dasa, Prem Kishor dasa, Haridas Thakur dasa, Sudama dasa, Rudranath dasa, Rasikacharya dasa, Rasika Raman dasa, Vrajaraj Priya dasa, Nanda Gopa dasa, and hundred more have been a constant source of support and love.

My dear friends Anand Vrindavan and his wife Tulasi, Jigar Rawal, Gautam, Jahanavi, Rajan and Mita Padia, Palak and Paulomi Mehta, Rishab Goradia, Murari Nitai, Manasi Radhika, Dipti, Manisha, Jagadish, Rahul Danait, Aishwarya, Vaibhav Gudi, Priya Manjari, Rasa Parayana, Gopi Manjari, Jigar and Manali Shah, Sameer and Meghana Thakkar, Shifali, Sai, Nischay, Jash Gadhvi, Sarang, Ritika, Ishaa, Suchita, Purva, Ruchita, Kadamba Van and his family, and many more have helped me in many ways.

There are many other members of ISKCON community, both in Mumbai and all over the world, who by their constant support and encouragement have helped me in my spiritual life. In their association, I have learnt many aspects of spiritual life.

Gauranga Darshan, Amarendra, Nitai Sevini, Gaur Vilas, and others have nourished me with their devotional presentation of *Śrīmad-Bhāgavatam* and other scriptures.

Therefore, what you read in this book are not my realizations alone; it is a compilation of all that I have heard, read, and learnt from many devotees, friends, and guides, over the last two and a half decades. My heartfelt gratitude to all of them for their decades of silent dedication, steadfast commitment, and unceasing love and affection they shower on an insignificant soul like myself.

Finally, my sincere thank you to you for accepting this book.

JAICO PUBLISHING HOUSE

Elevate Your Life. Transform Your World.

ESTABLISHED IN 1946, Jaico Publishing House is home to world-transforming authors such as Robin Sharma, Sadhguru, Osho, the Dalai Lama, Deepak Chopra, Eknath Easwaran, Paramhansa Yogananda, Devdutt Pattanaik, Radhakrishnan Pillai, Morgan Housel, Napoleon Hill, John Maxwell, Brian Tracy, and Stephen Hawking.

Our late founder Mr. Jaman Shah first established Jaico as a book distribution company. Sensing that independence was around the corner, he aptly named his company Jaico ('Jai' means victory in Hindi). In order to service the significant demand for affordable books in a developing nation, Mr. Shah initiated Jaico's own publications. Jaico was India's first publisher of paperback books in the English language.

While self-help; religion and philosophy; mind, body and spirit; and business titles form the cornerstone of our non-fiction list, we publish an exciting range of current affairs, history, biography, art and architecture, travel, and popular science books as well. Our renewed focus on popular fiction is evident in our new titles by a host of fresh young talent from India and abroad.

Jaico's translations division publishes select bestselling titles in over 10 regional languages including Gujarati, Hindi, Kannada, Malayalam, Marathi, Tamil, and Telugu. These include titles from renowned national and international authors like Sudha Murthy, Gaur Gopal Das, Swami Mukundananda, Jay Shetty, Simon Sinek, Ankur Warikoo and Jeff Keller.

Visit our Website

Boasting one of India's largest book distribution networks, Jaico has its headquarters in Mumbai, with branches in Ahmedabad, Bangalore, Chennai, Delhi, Hyderabad, and Kolkata. This network ensures that our books reach all parts of the country, both urban and rural.